Say It Ain't So
"Say It Ain't So"
Say It Ain't So

Authoress Terry E. Lyle

TERRY E. LYLE IS BACK TO TAKE YOU ON ANOTHER JOURNEY INTO THE MIND WHERE SHE UNLOCKS THOSE HIDDEN PLACES. FOCUSING ON THINGS SECRETLY PUSHED WAY BACK INTO THE CORNER OF YOUR MIND, SO AFTER READING, I'M SURE YOUR RESPONSE WILL BE; "OH NO….SAY IT AIN'T SO"!!!

Order this book online at www.trafford.com
or email orders@trafford.com

Most Trafford titles are also available at major online book retailers.

© Copyright 2010 Terry E. Lyle

All rights reserved. No part of this publication may be reproduced, stored in a retrieval system, or transmitted, in any form or by any means, electronic, mechanical, photocopying, recording, or otherwise, without the written prior permission of the author.

Printed in Victoria, BC, Canada.

ISBN: 978-1-4269-3126-0 (sc)

ISBN: 978-1-4269-3127-7 (hc)

ISBN: 978-1-4269-3128-4 (e-book)

Library of Congress Control Number: 2010905553

Our mission is to efficiently provide the world's finest, most comprehensive book publishing service, enabling every author to experience success. To find out how to publish your book, your way, and have it available worldwide, visit us online at www.trafford.com

Trafford rev. 5/3/2010

Edited by Tracy Duke Arnold & The Authoress

 www.trafford.com

North America & international
toll-free: 1 888 232 4444 (USA & Canada)
phone: 250 383 6864 ♦ fax: 812 355 4082

AS A SPECIAL TREAT LOOK PAST THE TABLE OF CONTENTS TOWARDS THE BACK OF THE BOOK TO FIND THE APPENDIX WHICH WILL SHOWCASE UNKNOWN POETS IN HOPES OF THEM RECEIVING RECOGNITION THAT'S LONG OVERDUE. ALL WORK SUBMITTED WAS APPROVED AND PERMISSION FOR USE WAS GRANTED BY THE WRITERS WITHOUT MONETARY GAIN "BEFORE YOUR DREAMS CAN BE REALIZED AND

TERRY LYLE

MATERIALIZED YOU HAVE TO FIRST BELIEVE AND STEP OUT ON FAITH.

Welcome To My World

As You Read This
Fascinating Book
Titled
Say It Ain't So!!!
It Will Contain A Collection
Of Essays Sprinkled
With Truth And
Clarity With Profound
Wisdom That
You Can't Ignore
It Will Speak To Your
Inner Being, So Relax,
Enjoy, And Relate. Peace
And Blessings But
"Oh No_ Say It Ain't So"

TERRY LYLE

Relax And Relate

(DON'T PUT THIS BOOK DOWN, PICK IT UP, START READING, BUY IT, LISTEN TO YOUR INNER VOICE, YOU'RE JUST GOING TO LOVE IT!)

PREVIOUS REVIEWS

#1 Ms. Lyle captures the real emotions felt very candidly while her books are truly thought provoking and refreshing to read. Former retired Army linguist & nurse, Baltimore, MD.

#2 Ms Lyle's writing style is refreshingly genuinely honest and to the point. Public Speaker, Fort Lauderdale, Florida

#3 Ms. Lyle is definitely an interesting writer, such an enjoyable read her last publications. Brown Bag Poetry and Wow!!! (Windows of Wisdom) were a pleasant surprise. Retired Mass Transit worker, San Diego, California

#4 Ms. Lyle is fast becoming one of my favorite authoresses in her writing styles that touches your emotions and make you take a hard look at yourself. Business owner and self-defense instructor, Brooklyn, New York

#5 Ms Lyle gets two thumbs up for revealing the facts. Los Angeles, California,   CIA Agent.

#6 Ms Terry E. Lyle's previous books were very encouraging and full of solutions to everyday problems that you encounter, truly looking forward to reading her latest work, submitted by a Tractor Trailer Instructor, Russell County, Alabama.

ABOUT THE AUTHORESS:

Terry is a funny lady who is warmhearted, opinionated, witty, bold and focused. She sets her standards based on the requirements of honesty, respect and integrity. She practices accountability in all aspects of her life. Terry hides her pain behind smiles and jokes and usually suffers in silence. Terry is adamant about her spiritual growth and worship, and fearlessly accepts her role in the direction of child development, knowing it takes a village to raise a child and boldly she takes on that challenge to impart her wisdom while she honors her church, family, and friends always with her time, support and loyalty. Terry Lyle is a multi-talented female whose kind and thoughtful but she can take it up a notch in her opinions and will stand her ground. You will come to understand why she called this book,

"Say it ain't So"

TERRY LYLE

Dedication:

To the glory of God who sustains me and keeps me from falling through his loving mercy and grace upon my life he rains down his blessings daily.

Knowing I'm unworthy and there's nothing special about me, or nothing that I could do or offer God yet, still God loves me and continues to show me favor.

To God is the Glory, forever and ever.

Amen! Amen! & Amen!

I would also like to acknowledge some of my dearest Baltimorean friends that by some typographical error were not mentioned in my previous book. This lovely lady's name is Eartie Morris-Tyler, and family Angela, Kershin and Donald. Also my friends from Columbus, GA …Janine Rupp and Eric Anthony… Brother and Sisters in Christ… Samuel & Felicia Alexander, Henry & Zara Parham, Jerome & Lisa

Parham, Michael & Sandra Henry, Joseph & Mable Colquitt, Curtis & Lillian Holt, Warren & Bessie Clark, Danny & Angelia Walton, and Tara Hall and the rest of the brethren.

Contents

1.	Say it ain't So	1
2.	My Stuff	2
3.	You Should Be Mine	4
4.	God's Love	6
5.	Time to Think	8
6.	When You're Living On The Edge	9
7.	Pot Holes	11
8.	Correctional Officer	13
9.	Are You Gay?	15
10.	Locked Up	16
11.	Where Were You When I Needed You?	18
12.	I Need a Sugar Daddy	19
13.	Hair Loss	21
14.	The Black President	22
15.	Call On Me	24
16.	Death	25
17.	Angel Package	26
18.	Perpetrators	27
19.	Break Through	29
20.	Second Chances	31
21.	Getting Older	33
22.	Sexual Appetite	35
23.	The Twinkle of God's Eyes	36
24.	Harry's Dream	38
25.	Frustration	40
26.	Tortured Soul	41
27.	I'm Sick of You	42
28.	Fat Guys	43
29.	Behind Closed Doors	44
30.	Silent Tears	46
31.	For The Sake of Your Love	49
32.	Surprises	51
33.	White Death	53
34.	Sweating Bullets	55
35.	Dangerous Package	56

36.	Friends When Everything's Gone	57
37.	The Game	60
38.	A Parent's Nightmare	62
39.	Spanking	64
40.	I Need a Mini-Break	66
41.	Striking Back	67
42.	Secret Lovers	69
43.	You Can Talk	71
44.	Suffering	72
45.	I Feel Like a Princess	74
46.	Wanted	76
47.	Sleeping With the Enemy	77
48.	Wrong Answer	79
49.	In The Secret of Your Mind	82
50.	Dad	83
51.	Forbidden Fruit	84
52.	The Change	85
53.	Adultery	87
54.	Are You Going To Hell?	88
55.	Trapped In a Maze of Drugs	90
56.	Letting Go	92
57.	Don't You Feel Stupid?	94
58.	Bad Odors	97
59.	You Don't Know Me	99
60.	Man Trouble	101
61.	If Walls Could Talk	102
62.	Nina And Derrick	104
63.	That's What You Said	105
64.	Road Rage	106
65.	Sliding On Thin Ice	108
66.	Raped	110
67.	Forgiveness	111
68.	You	113
69.	Racism Madness	114
70.	Secrets	116
71.	Growing Up	117
72.	You Tell Me You Love Me	119
73.	Being a Victim	120

74.	Advice For Young Ladies Dating	123
75.	Distracted	124
76.	Yelling Into The Silence	125
77.	Inspiration	126
78.	Alone	127
79.	Watch Out	129
80.	Pregnancy	130
81.	Giddy	133
82.	Website Friends	134
83.	That's The Way It Is	136
84.	Moochers	137
85.	I Can't Wait To See You	138
86.	Cute	139
87.	Two Souls	140
88.	I Give Up	141
89.	Respect	142
90.	Church	143
91.	Somebody Told You Wrong	144
92.	APPENDIX A *	146

Say it ain't So

"Say it ain't So" is the title of this book
It's uniquely refreshing
that you can't help but look,
while provocative and sweet
it's truly a treat
it's easy to read,
yet exciting and fun
you'll love this book
before you get done.
With its adult content
about relationships
gone bad
and how to pick up the pieces
when you're lonely and sad
with its medley of situations
that we all go through
this book will talk
to the inner part of you
and the reality is
it will ring true too
"So say it ain't So"
should be the book
that you choose"

My Stuff

My stuff that I write about may not be the best,
but I will write my stuff and I won't rest
until I kick out some sweet little ditty
and
hear your remarks "Oh that was pretty"
I will write about all subject matter
until something comes along
that
I think is better.
I'll be just kicking out the rhymes
which is something I do all of the time.
I have won awards
and
I have been recognized.
For my writing skills I have won some prizes.
My writing style is about keeping it real
I'm not a fake, I'm the true deal.
When I write there is no limit.
I'm in this game and I plan to win it
so
enjoy yourself while you read my stuff.
I'm sure you will say
"Ahhhh Shucks, now that's what's up."
The Authoress
Is making it plain, so come on

and jump on this thing.
This book you will enjoy the read
with no doubt indeed.
As I give you
my
personal guarantee.

TERRY LYLE

You Should Be Mine

Every time we're together it feels right. That's why I know you should be mine. We are two broken pieces molded perfectly into one, becoming a whole. Lost in your eyes whenever you're near, a range of emotions I feel lets me know it's different this time, and you should be mine.
On a rainy day I feel the sunshine of your heart. We're like a perfect match, finishing each other's words simultaneously; I count the hours until the next time we meet. I've given you my soul and you've given me yours. You know that you should be mine, we fell in love and who could blame us.
Life is ticking away and I want you to grow old together with me. Trust me to do all the little things that show I care, but in my heart you're already there, resting comfortable inside of me. I can't help but wish that I could make things different with the snap of my hand, and be there to catch you whenever you fall, so you don't experience pain at all.
How cruel can life be when you bring the love of my life, in proximity of me, just to find out that he's not free? I want to run away but in my heart you're mine, forever and always. I can't eat or sleep because I'm so into you, that without you I will suffer the loneliness, caught up in my fantasy of beautiful

dreams. This you can believe, I need a miracle because I know you should be with me. Even though you're still resting in my heart so comfortably.
I pray Lord why couldn't you be with me?

TERRY LYLE

God's Love

We just don't take the time to see just how good life is, even through what we call the difficult times. I was lying on my bed thinking initially about the things I didn't have, the things I wished I had, and not appreciating what I did have. Then I heard the news on the television about massive destruction and loss of life surrounding the earthquake in Haiti. I saw all those babies without parents who died in the aftermath of the earthquake. All of their possessions in a blink of an eye were ripped away from them with chaos everywhere. Watching in horror how the survivors were scattered about crying, digging out from the dirt, rubble and debris with a look of disbelief upon their faces. Their scrounging around for any sign of life or looking for just a precious drop of water tore through my heart. My own tears of shock and dismay flowed uncontrollable down my face. With a sickening feeling of disgust at my own whining hit hard in the pit of my stomach.

I immediately began to pray fervently for help for the survivors and beg forgiveness for my own selfishness. I then looked around and thanked God for my life, my shelter, my family and for the ability to still feel compassion for someone else. I thanked God that I wasn't homeless today, because I've been there and for his mercy and grace upon my life. I can't stress enough that through it all God still provides. Even when you think God has abandoned you, just know he's still on the throne, and he'll never leave you. The thread of life is so intricately woven together that everything has a purpose, whether we see it or not, from God's master plan. Even in death, there springs forth new life. When you've had enough of the problems of this world, God's there to comfort you or bring you home to suffer no more. I pray that compassion, humility, and love never leave you and that you retain the ability to feel sorrowfully for someone else because in that moment, you'll begin to grow and mature in wisdom, and show the spiritual side of your existence.

Let there be no mistakes and know faithfully that God's love will sustain you. I know that, "My good days outweigh my bad days, and I won't complain".

Time to Think

It's good to have time to think, it helps you access what's going on around you, what works and doesn't work in your personal space. Everything is clearly understandable because the fluff and pretense is gone; leaving brutally raw truths to speak to your mind, while revealing and dissecting the reasons why you stayed caught up in someone else's role of acceptance. Inside you knew that you might have had fewer struggles doing things your way, if you had stuck to your decisions without constantly wavering. When does compromising become a futile role that should be abandoned? What qualities do these other people in your life have that carries so much weight in your mood swings? Intensely affecting your aura into a state of depression because you express your displeasure at their behavior, "So what," I think why not let them get mad. Maybe they will realize that your world doesn't evolve solely around them, and then maybe you can find a glimmer of happiness more frequently. So I ask you…. "When are you going to take time to think?"

When You're Living On The Edge

When you're living on the edge
barely able to hold on
you have nothing
now your money is gone
Living day to day
with deep regrets
fear taking over
while you sweat
How far can you go
before falling in
to
that nightmare world
full of sin
When you're living on the edge
there is no pretense
your life is rough
yet very intense
when you're living on the edge
With nowhere to turn
to
running to church
because your spirit is hurt
When you're living on the edge
and your choices are few

TERRY LYLE

you're still
hoping for a new opportunity
that's waiting for you
When you're living on the edge
Is the thing that you do
keep holding on tightly
So you won't slip over
too.

Pot Holes

I was riding down the street and there was a jerk.
My car shifted, then I smirked "What was that?"
I wanted to see and it turned out to be,
another pot hole,
facing me.
The streets were in need of dire repairs,
Potholes were noticed everywhere.
Driving has turned into an obstacle course,
where you keep
trying to avoid your cars from making
detours
into a funky ditch, avoiding
potholes which will make you switch
your lane of traffic really quick
so that pothole you avoid and do not hit.
I was driving down the street, singing my tunes
when my car started to dip way to soon
into another pothole I had hit
now my car needs to be fixed.
You won't get reimbursed when
you mess up your car
you would fare better ordering a drink from a bar
The city hasn't taken time to fix the stuff.
Whether you stomp your feet
or huff and puff
Somebody needs to show me

TERRY LYLE

where my tax money goes,
Because it can't be on fixing these potholes
and If so it doesn't even show.
Every time I turn around, some street needs repair.
Why won't the city buy asphalt and
pull the brothers from jail?
Putting that cheap labor to work would be fair
as they beautify the town everywhere.
I'm so sick of seeing these potholes around, the
city needs to correct this problem and do it now.

Correctional Officer

I was looking through the window pane and what I saw drove me insane.

There were people out there fighting, one was kicking and one was biting.

Blood was splattered everywhere, and the on-lookers shrugged their shoulders and didn't care.

My heart fell to my stomach watching this chaos, I wanted to vomit.

Why are things so out of control with continued lawlessness now taking its hold? Now decent people are acting insane, just like in the beginning with Abel and Cain.

People are mean and very bold; shamelessness has taken over control.

No respect could I see while I was looking through this window, when someone shouted and glanced at me. I felt danger in a horrible way knowing in this place I couldn't stay.

The alarms were going off and I couldn't hide, I had to get ready to flee quickly outside, I started running very fast, because now I saw a convict who was chasing my ass. Being a Correctional Officer will end today; if I survive this riot then I won't stay. Seeing anger directed at me only because I wear this uniform and I'm called security.

Are You Gay?

(My Inquiry of the gay and lesbian lifestyle)

Are you gay, and have you ever thought about it? It seems to me that a lot of phony people out there waste their time bashing people's lifestyles. Let's look at this realistically, I'm sure that at least 90% of the population has encountered lesbianism or homosexuality a little closer to home than they realize. First let's be honest, you know someone in your family tree is like this. Every family has a drunk, a loudmouth and closet queen or out the closet homosexual. Honestly I commend them for having the courage to live life the way they see it, and not be restrained by society's limitations. If you look a little closer you might agree that, the thought whether brief or not has crossed your mind at one time or another. Being homosexual doesn't mean they love less, work less or deserve less. Everyone has something to offer and should be treated with dignity. I embrace my homosexual family and friends because my mind isn't limited. How about yours? Have you hugged a gay person today? Or are you still in the closet of your mind trying to get out?

TERRY LYLE

Locked Up

The dreaded phone call
That no one wants to hear
came from me and was replaced by fear.
Locked up and I wondered what to do
I've made my call,
it's up to you
whether you come at all.
You're my ball and chain;
I'm the one who's mentally insane.
While I sit with nothing to do
I want to be bailed out pretty soon.
I didn't have God in my life,
There was no room
and I wouldn't even sacrifice
but now,
I pray and pray and pray.
Locked up from bad choices I've made,
leaving disgrace upon my family's face.
I stayed in trouble it always seems that I
can't find a way to keep my hands clean.
Hanging out with my home boys,
with our dangerous metal toys,
all kinds of guns throughout the house
when I was busted by The Vice.
I'm locked up and looking at time

I didn't even receive a dime.
So I guess I feel stupid now,
now I'm stuck doing this bit;
being incarcerated makes me sick
I might be mad as I roll my head
but blood's been spilled and another's dead.
I'm locked up and mad as can be,
beware if I'm around your family.
I'm bad and that's how it is
So you need to step off
before you're dead.
But this is the life I chose for me,
bad to the core is what you'll see

Where Were You When I Needed You?

Where were you when I was flat on my back?
Needing a friend to take up the slack.
Where were you when I was caught in the rain?
I was waiting on you and filled with pain.
Where were you when I buried my dad?
I was grief stricken and really sad.
Where were you on holidays past?
You were vandalizing cars and breaking out glass.
Where were you when I was rocking in pain?
I was left alone and feeling disdain.
Where were you when I needed some help?
After falling down on one of my steps.
Where were you when my car broke down?
You were hanging with friends
on the other side of town.
Where were you when I needed
to borrow some cash?
You were hiding in your house,
while smoking some hash.
Where were you when things fell apart?
You were still right there
buried deep in my heart.

I Need a Sugar Daddy

You came over here requesting my body, expecting something and being real naughty. You're not my sugar daddy, and you don't finance me, so knuckleheads get a grip, because I'm fancy free. You are calling me late at night; you must be crazy or want to fight. Your pockets are empty and you're not spending any cash, are you delirious, or are you smoking grass? You know that you're not in my league so stop trying to associate and pester me. You won't get anywhere, unless you have money that you're willing to share. "Otherwise get out of my face, because I really don't care." If you thought you were going to get this derriere wet, it would be a mistake that I haven't made yet. You know somebody must have told you wrong….crazy man, "why don't you go home." I'm looking for a sugar daddy that's willing to impress, knowing it takes money for me to look my best. I know my body is enticing, you obviously know this is true, because you're still in my face and you're acting a fool? Your time has passed to step up your game; your maneuvers towards me are totally lame. When I hear your voice on the phone, I'll tell you don't bother and please stay at home. Worry someone else and leave me alone. I'm sick of you and I'm sick of your voice, when it comes to sugar daddies, you're not even a choice. A Sugar Daddy is what I'm still looking for, please don't bother or knock on my door unless you're willing to offer me more.

Hair Loss

You're losing your hair, and it looks bad to you, it's
receding so far back you don't know what to do.
You have tried different ointments
and hair grows shampoos.
Nothing is working and you look crazy too.
When you look at your head and you
see it's a mess, beauty shops are making
a killing trying to cover the rest.
You've tried hair dyes to cover the bald,
put on wigs, you've tried it all.
Hair loss is a terrible thing, yet without it we feel
old it seems. Youth is fleeting and it goes by real
fast, you wish at least some hair would last.
You hate to see your hair turn gray or fall out
because it will not stay. It resembles a rabbit
that's running fast chewing on hair carrots. When
you comb your hair you're afraid to look, to see
how many strands that your comb has took.
So while you're thinking about your hair loss today,
why not try to figure out how to make your hair
stay, on top of your head nice and thick, instead
of thin and bald which is making you sick.

TERRY LYLE

The Black President

The Black President stood tall and wise
Representing our country with dignity and pride
The Black President
Gave hope to our youth
That they may reach for the skies,
whatever they choose
The Black President
Has a long road ahead
Knowing there are people out there,
that wish he were dead
The Black President
Has made a big change
With previous policies that made the country insane
The Black President
Stands for each one of us
Whites, Blacks, and the Minority sects
The Black President
Is a Godly man
Working to heal our country and heal our land
The Black President
Has a lot on his plate
Revising health care issues, that really can't wait
The Black President
Needs to be guarded
By Homeland Security

Who acts real retarded,
Allowing unknown guest
To be in his space,
What kind of crap is that?
It's a total disgrace!
The Black President
Is constantly under attack
Because of his skin and that is a fact
For years white America ran the show
They held the reins tight
And wouldn't let it go
The Black President
gave this country a jolt
with the biggest turnout in the history of votes
The Black President
is an honorable man
can change things around
as we see that he can
The Black President
They call him Obama
Gave hope to the world
and
Black babies' mommas

TERRY LYLE

Call On Me

Call on me when you need a friend,
I'll be there until the very end.
Call on me when you're all alone,
I'll stay with you and won't go home.
Call on me for all of your needs,
I will be there, yes indeed.
Call on me when you're feeling low
you can share your problems
And that you know.
Call on me in the wee hours of the night
that would be fine, and that's alright.
Call on me when you need to cry
I'll listen intently as you tell me why.
Call on me when you don't feel well
vomiting inside a bucket or pail,
while experiencing what feels like hell.
Call me when you need a hug,
because you were frightened, after you saw a bug.
Call me when you need a ride
I'll come to be there by your side.
Call on me anytime you like
because we're so close it would be right.

Death

Family death took me away from here,
now
death brought me back again this year.
I didn't want to stay in town
with constant bad memories still around.
I couldn't let my demons stay buried
now dug up
I'm living my life in a hurry.
It's hard trying to get a grip
now
that I realize on the medical tip
I won't make it back for another
trip.
I realize I'm going to die this year
so
I want to make it all crystal clear
and
come visit the friends of my past
because
my life is short and will not last.
I have cancer spreading fast
that's how I know my life won't last
and soon it will consume all of me
and
I hope my death leaves fond memories.

TERRY LYLE

Angel Package

They say that angels walk among us
do you know who they really could be?
It's even possible that angel
is me.

Packaged like an ordinary man
helping people where ever they can.
Angels could be that overlooked person
standing over there simply conversing.

Angels speak wisdom into your soul
they have lived a long life
from the beginning I'm told.

I'm watching the destruction of today
Angels came to earth to take pain way.
In other cases
they still will come
to escort you home where you belong.

Since the beginning of time,
Angels have always been around
coming to earth is their mission
fulfilling the plan of
God's holy vision.

Perpetrators

I'm trying so hard to get over you in my mind, while still laying with that miserable guy of mine that you called my partner in life. In the beginning it seemed that my whole world evolved around this person, who meant so much to me back then. Yet today I wonder how to get out and run fast in the other direction. Financial woes have me trapped. I'm caught accepting a loveless routine existence, filled with periodic sex once or twice every two weeks. My blood boils for the excitement of a heart-stopping, passionate, romantic lovemaking session. I find myself daydreaming and focusing on the ambience and romance in the air. I'm sick and tired of the routine; that signal of an occasional hug or leg thrown over top of mine which is the clue that I may get lucky tonight, because sex won't be denied. It'll last twenty minutes tops then another routine will begin, grab a tissue, wipe it off and go to sleep. Frustrated and lacking the intimacy that should accompany the love. Sex has become a reward if I don't get on my partner's nerves. The sparkle is fading and I indiscreetly look around to find someone else. I wish I could find that person to fill the spark of excitement of days gone by. Often I find myself casually reminiscing of the happiness of my past, with eyes open wide and frozen in time. Suddenly I've notice a scent familiar to me, as it crosses my nose and ignites the fire that's dying inside of me. Now I'm optimistically feeling hopeful while contemplating how to perpetrate situations in my favor and with whom.

"Will I get caught if I try to cheat or act naïve when I know someone is trying to seduce me?" I thought that you would be with me forever, but now the yearning is focused into another direction. My loins ache with the thought of unbridled passion, and I'm willing to cheat for just a few moments of escape into the arms of another who wants me there. The chemistry and heat rises whenever I catch the smile or glance in my direction of the lover waiting in the wings for me to come to them. We are unbridled and courageous in our secret longing to tear each other's clothes off, while keeping that appropriate distance. I find excuses to be where you are so I can sneak a hug or close embrace of greeting, while I close my eyes and stick you into my memory banks; I know that our brief moment has to last for what seems like a lifetime. I rehearse silly things to say when I want to call you, perpetrating excuses so I can hear your voice.

When I hear your laughter, I visualize your face and body that I long to embrace as my body tingles at the sound of your voice. "Is this my own personal madness caught between lust and lies while I continue to perpetrate?"

Break Through

I'm looking for a break through
from poverty to prosperity
I've spent everything that I had.
This is my dream and I'm not sad,
because I'm waiting on my break through.
From fat to skinny as I start thinning,
building my confidence and I'm winning
while I'm waiting on my break through.
I'm looking towards wellness from illness
with more good days, "I'm feeling this"
as I wait on my break through.
Getting my grades and I'm not afraid,
because college is a step away; I'm
sitting here waiting on my break through.
My relationship was bumpy
and my head was lumpy
and being abused was old news
while I was waiting on my break through.
Kids are rotten and sometimes forgotten
when they are acting bad, and making you mad
you need to wait on your break through.
Family members mooching on you
you can't wait until they move
you focus on staying calm through the storm
while waiting on your break through.

TERRY LYLE

Car breaks down and you're out of town.
Insurance expired
and you're real tired
as you wait on your break through.
now who shows up in the nick of time
when you're down to your very last dime?
My name is called Break through.

Second Chances

Second chances I've had a few, but if I were
honest with myself I'll still need more too.
My life is constantly revolving around the
madness from which I'm trying to escape.
I'm trying to be good when I feel emotions
of rage and thoughts that appears evil.
That is why I'm sure I will need a second
chance. The first time I vow never to sleep
With someone else's man, I'll try for a season, but
lust might be the reason I'll need a second chance.
The next time I vow not to be late, and I have
you irritated while you wait. That will be a time
when I'll need a second chance at forgiveness.
I've never claimed to be perfect, I'm just who
I am. Flaws included, and I don't want to be
excluded, I just want another second chance.
If I promise to give you the whole world, but
fall short and you'll only make it to New York,
this is when I'll need a second chance.
I will promise you endless days of splendor,
as I watch you cry when the house is
repossessed by the lender. This will be a
time that I will need a second chance.
I vow to be there in sickness and in health,
but when you were laid up hurt

TERRY LYLE

I was somewhere else.
This would be a time I would need a second chance.
When I've made a complete mess of my life
I'll know what to do, I'll get on my knees
and beg and plead
praying fervently
as I bow down to you LORD
and ask for a second chance.
because
You're the God of Second Chances.

Getting Older

Just because I'm getting older doesn't mean I
don't feel vibrant anymore. Getting older makes
me appreciate the special times and moments.
Getting older doesn't mean that I don't
want to fall into love or feel love.
More than ever before, I want to feel
needed, pampered, nurtured and sexy.

Getting older only means, I'm still as sharp as
I was mentally, but only physically slower.
My hair maybe trying to turn gray and my bones
may creak, and I might need sedatives to sleep,
but from my standpoint, life's been sweet.

Getting older doesn't mean I don't want to have a
good time, but if I'm alone then that's just fine.
Getting older doesn't mean I want to be lazy.
Even though I may help out
sometimes, don't get crazy.
Getting older doesn't mean I'm
going to accept just anything.
Getting older is a blessing.

Getting older allows me the time to
enjoy the impossible dreams,
of all the new things that I've seen.

TERRY LYLE

I'm getting older, and I don't know how long
I'll be here, but before I go, I need you to know
that through it all, the ups and the downs, it
always felt good to have my love ones around.

The world is constantly changing, you'll
need to learn to adapt, be flexible and not
carry the world on your back. Don't become
so stuck on all the old ideas of the past.
Focus on how to make morality last. Don't shut
your heart down, embrace a loving relationship,
and seek peace through a spiritual connection,
through a church of your choice is your selection.

Don't give up because you're slowing down,
Don't feel bad because your friends aren't around.
They may have gone on to glory,
but this is your story.
Live life and don't hesitate, put a smile
on your face you're still in the race.

Sexual Appetite

If you lose your sexual appetite what would you do?

Would you touch yourself or complain and stay blue?

Would you be happy without it at all, since you don't have anyone who even bothers to call?

Would you make excuses, because you don't like the way that you look?

Would you get creative and read an encouraging book?

Would you go see a doctor and find out what's wrong?

Would you blame it on your man, because he was gone?

Would you tell yourself that you don't need it anymore?

Or have those chapters in your life, you have closed the door?

The Twinkle of God's Eyes

Star-bright, starlight I wish I had some hope tonight.

I wish I had more money to spend, on my face would be a big grin. I want to be a happy soul before my body is buried and cold. I wish to be filled with love, which comes from God above.

Star-light and star-bright this is my only wish tonight. Tomorrow when I awake from slumber, my mind will be racing as I wonder. "Did God hear my prayer, or because of my sins, he chose not to hear?"

Maybe God wants me to turn to him. Knowing only he can forgive my sin, instead of me wishing upon a star I would have more luck trying to win a car. If I constantly kneel and pray I am sure things will go my way.

Star-bright and starlight I hope you're the twinkle in God's eyes tonight. What will life bring me today in a special crazy way? Even when things go wrong, we should fill our hearts with songs.

Sometimes the problems we have today are usually caused because we forget to pray. Never realizing what God blocks from our view, this concept is understood by just a few. Yet we continue on and never pray to remove the obstacles out of our way. So starlight and star-bright, fill my heart with agape love tonight.

Harry's Dream

For the longest that I can remember
I've had this friend named Harry.
I'm sure he's like other men,
quick fast, and scary.
They profess they will love you
unto their dying end.
This is the crap to be expected
from these types of men
Now Harry I couldn't trust as far as I could spit,
This cock roach he's full of tricks
hell
he was already living with another chick.
Pushy in wanting me to show him some affection,
Harry didn't get it that we didn't
have that connection.
Harry wasn't all that bad; he even made me laugh,
at different times when I felt sad.
Harry is a good friend that I wish the best
Harry is going to go undercover
when he goes out west.
When his money train comes in
he'll be surrounded by his new found friends,
just like the rest, so full of themselves
when they have a few ends left.
That buster will have to have a breakdown

before he thinks he's going to lay me down
　　　But only in his dreams
Will Harry get the chance to tap this thing?

TERRY LYLE

Frustration

Truly frustrated and pulling out my hair,
I feel so twisted; I should have stayed in bed.
I Feel like I'm having, a nervous break-down,
My face is wrinkled with several frowns.
My head is thumping and my eyes even hurt.
Conversations become irritable.
Being nice seems like work.
My jaw has tightened and they even hurt.
I'm kicking at the ground, I'm kicking the dirt.
Plus everyone around me is fussing real loud.
So I guess I'll throw my complaints
Into this noisy large crowd.
Popping aspirin doesn't seem to work.
My head is thumping and it really, really hurts.
I think I need to get back into bed,
So this frustration will stop the pounding inside of my head.
That's making me act so mean and so weird.

Tortured Soul

My soul is tortured since you've left, sneaking around with a girl name Beth. I trusted what I thought our life could be; now I have a hollow heart and my soul is empty.

Aimlessly I've tried to move on, but I can't think clear since you've been gone.

You kept me on hold when I wanted out, now it seems we scream and argue and fight.

The pain of heartache cuts real deep; my soul is tortured even in my sleep.

I know I should move on and it's hard to do, I think of these things when I look at you.

Call me stupid if you will, I loved you in the beginning and I always will.

Love is such a tricky game, it includes heartache and it includes some pain. But if the choice was up to me, I'd rather be loved than tortured and left lonely.

I'm Sick of You

I'm sick of you. I'm sick of sitting here waiting for you to show up and you never call. I know you didn't answer the phone when you noticed it was me, because you didn't want to explain where you were. Time and time again we've had this same conversation and all I get is empty promises of change that maybe last for a day or two while you take on a posture of this is who I am. I'm spinning my wheels vowing to put the negativity behind me, knowing all along I didn't trust the words as soon as I heard them, blinded by my love and familiarity. As the lies continued, the pleasurable moments that we used to share became brief, warm tender embraces in each other's arms. Now every small thing triggers arguments and I can't wait to say it's over, wondering why I stayed so long. I'm looking forward to the unknown without you, driven by the hope of excitement and the releasing of despair. It's going to be different without you, but I don't care I need a healthy relationship because "I'm sick of you".

Fat Guys

I like fat guys and they aren't that bad,
some are cute and handsome dads.
Fat guys are coddlers and lots of fun; you
won't see them on a track team because they
hardly run. Fat guys are soft and very warm
when they hug you with their hairy arms.
Fat guys are sweethearts and usually smart
and known for having a loving heart.
Fat guys really enjoy their food; they won't
turn it down because they think it's rude.
Fat guys will either treat you like a lady,
or treat you like their special baby.
Fat guys I really dig, they don't carry
weight resentment in their heads
They will accept you for who you are,
that's why they win my vote and all.
Fat guys can really dance; I found this out when
I had the chance. I was kicking it at this club one
night, fat guy showed up and things went right.
We were dancing like Ginger Rogers and Fred
Astaire; I sweated straight through my hair.
Now I really don't know much about you,
but
I like all men and fat guys too.

TERRY LYLE

Behind Closed Doors

Everybody has secrets that come out behind closed doors. People pretend this stuff doesn't happen but it does. Let me explain. Looking into my eyes you'll seek the sparkle of innocence, but did you know behind closed doors I'm into dominatrix, taking your money if the price is right, while making you my slave. I'm respected in the community and have a great job, but behind closed doors, I walk around nude and curse like a sailor, while watching pornography and getting off into my own masturbation.

Home alone behind closed doors, you will find the pretending is dropped, just like your clothes that you take off, like the hair, the prosthesis, and the teeth in a jar. Also behind closed doors you're a wife beater, but smile to everyone out in the public. You explain your partner's sickness and her swollen eyes by saying she's clumsy and has a bad habit of running into walls. Cleverly you state that the marks around her neck are from jewelry too tight. How ludicrous it is that you expect to be believed; her escape is inevitable, she waits for the right time to flee from behind those closed doors.

Behind closed door is human trafficking and drug distribution, cries of pain and torture, muffled by the loud sounds of music, and clouds of drugs being manufactured, while surveillance cameras are everywhere.

What's behind your closed door? The excitement of your wedding day being planned and airline tickets to make; girls giggling on the phone while texting, and young men sprawled out on the sofa making a mess and watching sports. Your house is jacked up and you're used to it. Behind closed doors are secret meetings of the dark side, covens, demons, and witches come together to drink blood and make sacrifices and scare the hell out of normal people. They build secret rooms to chant and worship the devil and call him from the pits of hell. They terrorize the neighborhood looking for victims to be kept, snatching them from behind closed doors.

Everyone does their best to put their best foot forward, but many secrets are hidden behind closed doors. Look at yourself in a mirror and you'll wish there were things you could change about yourself, but those desires remain dormant behind closed doors.

Silent Tears

All alone again, as the tears flow from my eyes, burning liquids leaves a trail upon my cheeks. My eyes sting when trying to focus and look past the well of sadness and loneliness. I'm too ashamed to admit the stupidity I feel in acknowledging I'm not as special as I thought I was in your life. I cling to the small show of affection because I crave to be needed as the center of their universe. Time and time again, the disappointments, lies, excuses, and calls never come. They leave me alone in the dark thinking depressing thoughts, while fighting back the silent tears that are winning the race down my face, only to be wiped away by the back of my hand in sorrow. Smiles are no longer on my face, replaced with sadness, and I call this love, with its touch of madness. I'm driven to those emotions that aren't pleasant and very intense; as my heart pounds in my chest, I wonder will it burst and explode into tiny fragments? What an ugly place I find myself in when there are silent tears. I'm all alone again and again, and now there are no excuses. The raw ugly truth that I try to deny exists; it's just what it is. As the tears fall from my eyes, with a deep breath, I wipe the moisture from my face and vow to never again play the role of the fool, with my silent tears betraying me. I have replaced sanity with screaming bouts.

I have menacing feelings like treading on thin ice and afraid I'm about to fall inwards into that dark hole of anger, rage and despair. The truth is found cloaked between the emotions hidden behind the silent tears. Honestly sometimes I feel the urge to hurt you and make you cry. Behind the silent tears are thoughts of revenge, which I could inflict at any moment. In your foolishness you continue to bait me to thoughts of getting even. I hate now when I fantasize about the good times and how my heart clings to those loose threads of false sentiments. I'm constantly discontent and losing all hope of change that you promise would be forth coming. I find myself wondering why I'm afraid to let go. I haven't forgotten how to play the game. I wasn't supposed to fall in love, but I did, now I'm stuck in limbo and won't venture into another direction because I'm unsure of whether I would have given up too soon. The path I'm on is shaky and filled with constant silent tears. I want adventure in my life, but I want a qualified co-driver to take this journey with me into Loveland, however all I have are my dreams that I cling to and my silent tears.

I play for keeps, but I need a show of commitment that I'm not in this affair alone. I don't need a relationship built on my lover bringing nothing to the plate except conversation, drama, and offers of sex which isn't special anymore. Should this relationship be based on freaky sex, screaming, and sweat attacks? When does the heart and mind get nourished? Shouldn't I require more for myself than what I've so willingly accepted? I blame others for having lack of standards, but I shut myself down and forget to adhere to the reason why I should be happy and act carefree. Everyone else does whatever they want and think that people should lap it up with eagerness because they showed their presence. Yet in my life my soul has been stored away, hidden in my closet of emotions, which I expose only when no one else has time for me. Shady people around me with their life filled with tears and drama dump on me and want me to become their buffer. Life has to be filled with more excitement for both persons. It's wrong to constantly let yourself become torn because you want to reach back and grab a hold to any extended hand in need. I always want to rescue and try to be the kind of person that's always there to assist, yet I'm all alone crying silent tears. The question now becomes whether this is worth it. The cleansing effect left behind from the silent tears will motivate me. I begin a new walk with my head held high with integrity, while not becoming the person that I despise, a heart that is callous, self centered, untrustworthy, and missing in action. Sometimes you just get tired of fighting and you need to move on. I vow to stop killing my spirit over someone whose not worthy of me because within my silent tears, I found me.

For The Sake of Your Love

For the sake of your love I would stay at home

Instead of thinking about cheating, everywhere that I roam

It wouldn't make any sense for me to hang in the streets

That would create a new problem, while being indiscreet

Not wanting to violate his trust, that's placed so deep in me

I'll give him all the best, so the whole world could see

My love for him is special and my love for him is true

To lie down my life for him, would be the easiest thing to do

For the sake of love I would hush my mouth

I wouldn't keep secrets from my unsuspecting spouse

For the sake of love I would do anything

Treat my husband special, and to him my heart I'll bring

TERRY LYLE

For the sake of love, I should make integrity key
So I can present freely, the best parts of me
For the sake of love I have given you this ring
We shall live happily ever after because
You're my king and I'm your queen.

Surprises

My day started out just like any other day. I thought about the things I wanted to accomplish and the anticipation of the surprises of the unexpected. Well, this day was extremely busy. I had numerous errands and chores to complete. Towards the end of the day, my body was sore and racked with pain. The only thing I visualized was getting into bed and hoping for sleep. I took a warm relaxing shower and crawled into bed. As I snuggled and positioned myself on my side of the bed, I felt the warmth of your body heat against my leg. Comfortingly I reached out and patted your leg in acknowledgement, as I rubbed softly the smoothness of your body hairs beneath my palm. My hands began to caress the texture of your skin, when I felt my heart begin to violently pound in my chest. Unable to catch my breath, within seconds I became aroused by your closeness and the yearning need for your hands to touch me. Secretly, the passion in me seemed enormous at that moment. Below the hum of the A/C unit, blowing its coolness upon my body, I turned to you and guided your hands to touch me. My flesh screamed out in hunger to be manipulated, pinched, and pulled. In mounting anticipation, my mind began to whimper tears of excitement when you plunged your manhood parts into me. My derriere started to slowly dance and move in perfect harmony towards your touch. So quickly I burst into flames that I hadn't realized that I had complained about being in pain and so tired earlier, but at that very moment my body was glowing and pain free. Every part of my body tingled with excitement. I leaned over to kiss your moist lips with the taste of your sweat upon my tongue, feeling totally satisfied. I rolled over to sleep which seemed like only minutes before the alarm clock rang out; it's time to get up. Smilingly I wondered what surprises I would definitely encounter on this day.

White Death

Snowflakes falling covering the earth in its blanket of white death. Forty-two inches of snow have turned the city into a ghost town. People are stranded in their homes and on their jobs.

There are no sounds of life to be heard anywhere. The homeless have turned their cardboard boxes into igloos to find heat in a blistering, unending storm. Everything is shut down, including stores and mail delivery. The birds are walking, looking for a place to nestle.

Phone lines are jammed and cable cords are snapping under the weight of the snow. Oil tankers are sliding off the highways to their death due to patches of black ice, while seniors are dying from the frigid coldness because of empty oil tanks that can't be filled to warm their homes.

Children are forbidden to eat the white flakes that have paralyzed the city. Neither are they allowed to make snow angels, for fear of the colds that they might catch. They will have nothing to soothe or warm their bones, as they tremble and cough with chills penetrating straight to their soul, falling victim to the white death.

White death, in its illusion of beauty, will make you shiver from hypothermia and replace your speech with coughs of congestion within your chest.

When the end approaches, the white light that people speak about could be the white death that eventually covers all in its trappings of beauty.

Sweating Bullets

I'm sweating bullets
because
I have a court date today.
How do I make this problem go away?
I wish I could run somewhere and hide,
but the marshals' are walking by my side.
I'm sweating bullets
can't you tell?
I hurt myself when I fell
into a pile of doggy crap,
slipping and sliding on my back.
I'm sweating bullets
before I get home,
I spent the rent money and now it's gone.
What will my husband say to me
when in
my responsibility
I failed miserably?

TERRY LYLE

Dangerous Package

I was attracted to your package. Your look, your smile, the whole total thing had me mesmerized. I couldn't wait to unwrap this package, not knowing behind those pretty eyes were lots of deceit and many lies. All he wanted was someone to stroke his ego, and like the saying goes, he turned out to be another beagle. A man who was nothing but a dog that flew under the radar and caught me off guard. I have learned to beware of the fancy package; his surprise for me was explosive plastics. Looking back, that was a long time ago. The damage on my face currently shows. Now no one is attracted to my package. My face is disfigured because of that bastard. He's still on the run from the law and I'm sure he's sitting in another bar, smiling lovely at someone else while waiting to ruin a life and leave it a mess. He hasn't been caught as of today, so sometimes when people smile at you; it's ok to just walk away. Emotional scars dampen your life and you can't move on. There is nothing ventured and nothing gained, but you'll maintain your sanity so you won't go insane. Looking over your shoulder and living in fear is what's left of my life after the tears. Be careful and beware when you open some packages, you might be unwrapping dangerous baggage. Take your time and see things through, do your research before his next victim is you.

Friends When Everything's Gone

Your life isn't what it used to be. Many variables have changed now it's replaced with panic and pain, without personal gain. In your life you're dealing constantly with stress and strain, while hopes and dreams are slipping quickly down the drain. Options or directions you won't need to take after the realization that everything's gone, because of your mistakes. Since putting things off and making people wait, now your life is a mess trying to fix it way too late. Caught in a comfortable lifestyle with seemingly smug deceit thinking everyone else was beneath your expensive feet. Spending money very cavalier even though due payment of bills were constantly near. Your gravy train has come to an end; even I've loss sympathy for the mess that you're in, because you didn't listen to me and you chose your old friends. You took their advice and now you can't win, with their hands stuck out still wanting to borrow, and you to lend. Often I've tried to warn you before things became worse, yet you glared at me with that same indignant smirk. I thought I would share my wisdom because of our bond, but you chose not to listen to me and now everything's gone. Now your life is hectic

and full of drama, no one can save you, except
God but not President Obama. Your relationships
are rocky and your friends are few, while behind
your back they are whispering all about you.
As long as the money train will continue
to flow, you'll feel superior to others
and it will obviously show.
Family members throw slurs and talk behind your
back, the proof is out there and it's definitely a fact.
The routine and laughter, the ups and the downs
and everywhere you go, there are fake friends
around. You finally get it now that you're all alone,
since your money is spent and everything is gone!
Now never take it for granted when you get a
real friend, they will stick by your side until
the miserable end. They will offer you support,
money, food, shelter and many different types
of things, this is what real friends do when
you've lost everything. So when you know
that you have at least a real friend, tell all the
phonies to get lost and start over again.

Your friend is someone who's willing to stand
beside you without greed on their mind; they
will be very supportive, strong, but yet not
unkind. When everything's gone they will help
you get back on your feet, a situation caused
by your drama and the mess of your defeat.
They might be a little harsh in sharing the truth,
but you will believe them this time because they

will offer you proof. So the warnings of life that you will need to heed, is to choose your friends wisely because enemies will flourish like weeds. Your so called friends will create contention behind your back, begging from you while you're under their attack. Just let your money start soon to disappear; those phony friends will dissipate quicker than drinking a beer.

Maybe one day we'll meet again when every thing's gone and you need a true friend.

The Game

Let me put you down on the game. Don't get it twisted, the players are different but the game remains the same. This advice is being offered so that you don't get hurt, or played, because if you mess around, you might get laid. So my brothers and my sisters, listen. You've heard what's been said, "A hard head makes a soft behind," and the words I share might not sound too kind. Sisters when the fellows that you happen to meet, even though they look cute and sound so sweet, may be planning to get you between the sheets, that's part of the game. If he really respected you as a woman, it would take more than a date, so your body you shouldn't give him; just make him wait. Sex is his objective and if he gets it on the first night, it won't be long before he takes flight. Don't become a booty call with benefits because you can believe that he won't remember it. If you don't care about being respected, then give him your body, but get ready to be rejected. You know it takes maintenance to keep your body fresh, if he's not willing to pay for it, then he's like all the rest. That's part of the game. If the fellow only visits late at night, trust and believe he's sneaking, trying to stay out of sight. This is part of the game, to get in where they fit in. My sisters know you won't be able to learn all there is in one day, the players have skills and they wait in lay. That's part of the game. When you're on the dance floor swaying to the beat and you're getting all caught up because of your body heat, that ain't love, that's just the game. Now for my naïve brothers, who can't believe they have a date with this hot female, you need to hear and obey; these females are trying to take your money away. You haven't been lucky before, they chose you because you were the score and that's part of the game. Didn't you know you had a bull's eye on your back; the ladies are trying to get you into the sack, that's part of the game. You thought that you fell in love at first sight, how often does that happen? You know that ain't right? But that's just part of the game. They will say what you want and do anything, and try to trap you into giving them a ring, and that's just part of the game. Also my brothers and sisters use protection, don't trust the line "I'm clean", because you can get an infection. So wear a condom for your protection. That's just part of the game. You might find yourself a brand new daddy, because the girl you slept with was trifling and nasty. You got tricked on a cheap thrill because she chose not to take her birth control pills and that's just part of the game. Last but not least there are many players and variations to the game, but one thing that will never change, respect yourself first and you're ahead of the game.

A Parent's Nightmare

Pacing the floor and unable to sleep, your child is missing and you cry and weep. Hours have passed and there is no word, you wonder and think about the last things you've heard.

Praying your child isn't dead or hurt, or buried somewhere beneath the dirt. The police have been notified and there's no news, as you wait frantically and you become unglued.

You've contacted the neighbors and all of their friends, soliciting help where ever you can. You become anxious as the hours pass on, day has changed to night and it's a brand new morn.

Watching the clock and pacing the floor, while constantly glancing towards the door. Your heart is broken and filled with dread, thinking over the possibilities in your head.

Where is my child, were they abducted by force? Thinking it's your fault, while feeling remorse. Calls coming in, but there is no news; wondering the next course of action to choose.

You find yourself down on your knees, begging to GOD to help you please. People gather in prayer along with you, because your child they don't want you to lose. However there is still no news, since your child has gone away, while you pace and sit and pray all day. Hoping your child will come home tonight so you can hold them, love them, and keep them in sight.

TERRY LYLE

Spanking

After the discipline "The love doesn't change".

I know you've received a spanking, but young man put that behind you and move forward in a positive way. The spanking was supposed to be a deterrent against repetitive negative behavior, however the love doesn't change.

You are talented and very gifted, and the learning begins now as a child, so that you may mature into a wonderful man someday. There are so many people including your relatives, friends of the family, neighbors, church, and school associates who love you and only want the best for your future; especially your parents, who wants that the most.

Grab a hold of all the educational opportunities and wisdom that life will expose you to. Also, strive for greatness even in the midst of the obstacles before you, my young innocent king. I pray for your present and your future endeavors. Young heart always be wise and listen to the truth you can feel in your spirit, even though life for you have only just begun.

May your spankings become internal and inflicted upon by your own thoughts? May you have the mindset and willingness to change your bad habits, so that physical discipline won't become a habit or problem for your care givers. Trust the wisdom of the adults that care for you, knowing your well being is their first priority. Learn respect as you show others respect for their time and intentions invested into you. Tomorrow's future is carved from the directions and investments of the past. Don't waste your opportunity at greatness because you want to act like a clown, unless you aspire to be in the circus.

I Need a Mini-Break

I'm happy to have a mini-break from work,
where I deal mostly with stupid old jerks.
The stress of my job really gets me down,
on my forehead is a permanent frown.
I'm always trying to beat the clock
so that my paycheck never gets docked.
This mini break is what I needed
to have some fun and act conceited.
I act like I own the world, while
licking my fingers and eating cheese curls.
I'm learning how to forget the drama
and watch TV about President Obama.
But as soon as I get back to work
I'm stuck with those same old jerks,
who whisper behind my back
they're always gossiping about this and that.
I truly need a mini-break
so my stress doesn't make me sully and hate.
Or is my life ruin and this is my fate?

Striking Back

I'm not going to tell you and you're not going to tell me. I'm just going to be what I need to be.

I have to make my own mistakes on this road of life, I'll consider your thoughts and I'll consider your advice.

I know I'm young and mostly naïve, but I want to be what I need to be.

I want to be respectful and I need to be free, from all this confusion that's surrounding me.

I won't live any longer in a house full of abuse, it don't make any sense that your mind you don't use.

Look at the example that you're setting for my life, am I doomed to act this way when I find me a wife?

You've hurt the family when you beat on my mom, now I have nightmares that frequently come.

I know I'm a young man starting out on my own, don't try to discourage me because I'm leaving home.

I know you think I'll be back in a week, but after looking at you, it's not me who is weak. Flaunting your masculinity by using your fist, watch yourself daddy before you have a death wish.

I've taken the abuse and it's taken so long, now I have the courage to move out and the courage to stay gone.

I will never try to hurt the ones that are special in my life; I will protect them and care for them, and make everything right. If you love someone then, it should be obvious that them, you don't fight.

Secret Lovers

With a smile on your face, you can't wait until the evening comes, where you can blend into the darkness with your secret lover. Sneaking around somehow seems worth it for those stolen moments.

Heart beating fast in anticipation of that meeting, where a stolen kiss, stolen embrace, or a stolen glance is all that's needed to put the biggest smile on your face.

Secret lovers living in sin, with adventures manifested in the mind and played out in the bedroom, traveling from hotel to motel and from place to place, hiding the affair that's leading nowhere except heartache and heartbreak, because you belong to another.

Secret lovers whispering words of enticements in your ears, while unappreciated at home, you crave the attention and passion from your secret lover. You hate to see the time ticking away on your clock, robbing you of precious moments left to spend with your secret lover.

Sneaking around and hiding gifts and calls made to your secret lover. Dreaming that things could be different, and thinking you've found the love of your life, when you've only found yourself lonely on holidays and the object of their sexual fantasy.

Secret lovers trapped in a web of lies, flying below the radar, while hoping their indiscretions stay hidden in the night.

You Can Talk

You can talk about you.
You can talk about me.
You can talk about your past.
You can talk about a relationship
that didn't last.
You can talk about your family.
You can talk about your friends.
You can talk about cursing
those low-down men.
You can talk about politics.
You can talk about the news.
You can talk about casinos
and the money you lose
But don't talk ill about my God
Because that's a topic I take real hard
I'm not trying to censor your tongue,
but if you get disrespectful then we are done.

Suffering

Your life is passing by while you suffer in silence in your home inside, needing joint replacement and going downhill, lack of medical coverage you require still. Insurance companies are giving you flak, knowing they should pay for your surgery towards your knees and back.

While you're waiting, other things tend to go wrong and now you're singing that same old song. Pain is a part of your life each day, and all you want is it to go away.

Depression has sat in and you think about checking out, knowing that's not the answer and knowing it's not right. Your family is struggling along beside you, while the pressure is building and you're feeling the blues. Your limitations have increased inside you feel rage like an angry beast. Lately everything's topsy turvy and you feel real crazy, because on the outside you appear to be lazy but you're suffering.

You've become dependent on others to do the smallest things, this is a result of what suffering will bring. Physical and mental suffering soon becomes friends as you look for relief that the medicines will bring.

Taking pain and sleep medicine so you can go out like a light, because all you do is toss and turn through the night. Trying to be nauseously optimistic, your insurance company isn't helping and that's realistic.

I Feel Like a Princess

Every little girl in her life has imagined being a princess before, waiting on prince charming. Recently I had a diva moment and the thoughts rocked my world. In the middle of the room was a canopy bed with the shear drapes hanging softly, while blowing slowly from the air circling inside of the room. Soft red lights set the mood of seduction and romance. Upon the bed were the comforter and pillows, scented from the aroma of one of my finest colognes. My body glistened from the water lying upon my skin like dewdrops, fresh and inviting. I lay waiting for the moment your breath and tongue would lick my pulsating flesh. The tingling inside my body escalated, as I waited and thought about your touch upon me, while my breathing became deep and shallow. I positioned myself upon the fluffiness of the comforter in my nudity, as I began to touch myself in anticipation of your arrival. My nipples grew harder with each touch of my fingers that were dancing in circles, like ice skating with skill around the rigid mountains of chocolate flesh. "Oooh," I whispered as my body began to ignite into hot creamy moisture, needing to explode, while releasing the pressure building inside of me. I turned my head to the side where I saw your figure slowing approaching me, standing there fully nude and your manhood erected in excitement. I gasped with longing as you climbed into the bed to ravish me, while I opened my legs wider to give you a glimpse of my secret treasures. I closed my eyes because I felt like a princess with my prince upon me, feeling an illusion of grandeur as I smiled and remembered it was one of those diva moments. Sexual intensity completely satisfied in my canopy bed where often "I feel just like a princess."

Wanted

Are you wanted and are you hiding from the Feds'?

You have escaped from prison because you shot someone dead.

Beware there's a fugitive that's on the run, so lock your doors because a madman may come.

Home invasion is the way they will choose in efforts to hide from bulletins and news.

They have snuffed out a life of someone innocent and young.

Now a vigilante wants to pull the trigger from their personal gun.

When you're wanted there is nowhere to hide.

The bounty hunters will get you with the law on their side.

You are wanted, and let there be no mistakes, your freedom from you they will gladly take.

You're a pain to society, and the fear that is known, it's the stress we all feel until the law sends you home.

In the penitentiary is where you belong, where we house the rejects of society, that's where you should roam.

Sleeping With the Enemy

When you wake up and shake your head clear
Dread sinks in as well as fear
Looking at that monster still laying beside you
You want to kill her while she lay there and snooze
Your freedom, you ponder, you can't afford to lose
Your finances have dropped to an all time low
She stole it all, right underneath your nose
Beautifully she smiles while ripping you off
Your warning signs you've missed
 Now that she is your boss
She took your cash and she took your house
Now she snarls at you like you're the louse
You thought together that you would grow old
But that heifer stole your money, while acting bold.
She knew your account numbers and she knew them all by heart
On your bank account she made an assault
She was conniving and conning and twisted in her head

TERRY LYLE

Now all you wish is that soon…
That heifer drops dead.

Wrong Answer

How many times do we give out the wrong answers?

Let me tell you a funny story about me. A long time ago in my early twenties, I went looking for a job at an Alarm Company, no names please, I feel silly enough just remembering this funny story. Well I was prepped and ready to go on my job interview. I was early and well groomed. I had been told on several occasions that I have a pleasant personality, while being educated and a graduate, I knew this job was in the bag.

Eventually the time came for the aptitude test and I was speeding right along and one of the first to complete my test. I was beaming brightly because I had finished early and was waiting to be called in the back. Now to keep you abreast with me, let me explain what later my downfall became. There on this test was a fill in the box section, and one of the questions was "Fill in a fourteen letter word that would describe a person in charge of a plant." Now this is where things get good, I'm ecstatic because I knew the answer and I heard other people mumbling about the fourteen letter question.

As big as life, I proudly put down horticulturist, knowing I was in the game because after all, my entire life was watching mom who has a green thumb. All she did was plant and play in her garden and sometimes

I would have to carry large bags of soil and help dig. While never finding any use for such a back breaking experience, I finally beamed with pride how that little tidbit of knowledge finally paid off because, in fact, that's what my mom's part-time job was.

My moment finally arrived and they called my name. While looking back at those losers still taking their test, I strutted like a proud peacock to the back waiting area for the private interviews and to hear the good news. The first manager came out smiling, shaking my hand and asked me to have a seat and if I didn't mind she wanted some other staff members to sit in on the hiring process. One by one five additional staff members came in shaking my hand and smiling, so I just knew I had this job in the bag. I was complemented on my appearance and likeability factor, and was told that it was time to review the results of the test.

The head or lead manager stated she wanted to go over the question with the fourteen letter answer. I was asked how I was able to come up with that answer because usually that's the one left blank. So proudly I explained that my mom always took care of plants in her garden or house. To my surprise, everyone busted out laughing so heartily that I had to laugh too. And shortly after that is when the bomb fell. I was told that the answer they were looking for was superintendent and that they would definitely have to rewrite the test because my answer was also correct. However, for the job at an Alarm Company I was thinking too far out of the box. I saw a few of them wipe tears from their eyes because they were laughing so hard.

I graciously got up, shook their hands, smiled, said thank-you for their time, and left. When I got to my car I felt real stupid and cursed the fact that I thought I had an epiphany. Well I finally arrived home and my older sister Sylvia asked how my interview went. I told her what happened and she bugged her eyes out and started laughing and said "You really are a stupid, dumb nut," and walked away.

The moral of this story is, "When one door closes, another one opens." That same year I passed the test to become a Paramedic for the Baltimore City Fire Department. From there I went on to receive several commendations and had an award ceremony in my honor from the Mayor of Baltimore who, at that time, was Mr. Donald Schaefer.

So my real epiphany turned out to be "Never give up on a dream because you experience a few nightmares along the way".

In The Secret of Your Mind

In the secret of your mind is where I dwell, your secret story I need to tell. How longingly you crave to touch me from head to toe, caressing my body with your deliberate flow.

My breast you'll suck and my back you'll hold, as the heat and chemistry between us continue to flow. Sweat beads roll down my back as you take me so savagely in your lustful attack.

My legs you'll lick down to the top of my toes. My body will tremble and pulsate with glee, as your hands touch skillfully all over me.

In the secret of your mind you will need to awake and dream of me later before it gets late. There's a part of me that you hold very dear, it's that secret place where you tremble in fear, afraid to explode in a sexual lust, while longing to taste my voluptuous bust.

But for now I'll be the secret in your mind, as that will change a little over time. You're drawn to me like a moth to a flame seeking the encounters so wild and untamed.

Dad

Dad I miss you and I remember your smile.

Dad I miss you because you were my pal.

Dad I cry sometimes late at night, missing your comfort that felt just right.

Dad how can I go on without you in my life? I need you so badly for your loving advice.

Dad the seasons have changed and now I'm grown, I still miss you so deeply, right down to my bones.

Sickness took you away from those of us that's left here, dad we miss you each passing year.

Dad it's your birthday and I'm visiting your grave, remembering what you taught me and trying to be brave.

Dad I've learned so much from you, I pray I turn out as a man like you.

A loving father, teacher, and friend, Dad my love for you will never end.

Forbidden Fruit

Sex is the forbidden fruit you always
have to hush when the topic comes up;
when you're in cahoots in some people's
language it's called knocking the boots.
You act phony as if you hate it, but you're here
because someone mated. You act like you
forgot how good it felt and now the people
who like it, you think they need some help.
Sex it's been around far too long and it will
be around when you're gone. Your body
is yearning for sweet relief, being satisfied
by yourself while being discreet.
Hot and saucy in a rhythmic flow, bodies
swaying under a glistering glow. Together
you're stuck as if molded into one; all is right
with the world until your orgasms are done.
Feeling guilty about the forbidden fruit, having
sex without commitment will have you worried
and spooked. Now you may feel dirty and cheap,
because someone used you up and now you weep.
You had to have that forbidden fruit, while you try
to rationalize in your mind, why you've been cut
loose. How useless you feel, now that you know
it's real when it became apparently clear that your
lover saw your body…. as a necessary thrill.

The Change

Forget the world you came from and
embrace the world you're in,
that's how you will survive the
Change when it begins.

Blurring the lines of reality is not the way to do it,
you're going through menopause,
so you need to get used to it.

When you have hot flashes
and sweat like a pig,
wipe your face and snatch off your wig.

Cool your body temperature off
as quickly as you can,
use a fan or use your hands.

Menopause will have you ripping off your clothes,
and with your shoes, you'll stop wearing hose.
One minute hot and the next minute cold,
making you so mad, you hate getting old.

You will start acting like a crazy man,
this is part of the menopause plan.
Hormones are raging and out of sync,
going through the Change really stinks.

TERRY LYLE

The Change has lasted longer than you expected,
but for the record,
It made my life hectic.
Mood swings were out of control
as my body temperature changed from hot to cold.

Adultery

Adultery doesn't start in the sheets; it starts with hiding thoughts and being discreet.

Adultery is exciting and full of thrills, as you think about that person, which sends you a chill.

You hope for the moment that your secret is safe, while you long for some sweet embrace.

Your loins are on fire and your heart beats fast, your eyes light up like sparkling glass.

When you see that person of your desire, everything stops and your heart's on fire.

You're mesmerized by the look on their face, wanting to kiss them in a passionate embrace.

Knowing real soon, you'll be between the sheets, explosive intensity of your body heat.

Bolder you become in your approach, ready to move forward is all that you hope.

That day has finally come, and you make your move, swaying to the rhythm in a sexual groove.

Filled with shame about what you just did, you committed adultery, now your marriage is dead.

TERRY LYLE

Are You Going To Hell?

The end of days is near. Armageddon is around the corner with constant warnings predicting global warming, earthquakes, and natural disasters. Living in a society with shameless people having no respect for others or themselves, children are killing their parents and their classmates. Babies' are sodomized and raped, and human life is lost over a nickel bag of drugs.

Living in a shameless society where no one cares as long as you keep your mess in your yard. "Jesus is coming soon, so get ready," is the message of today. Having a spiritual conversation that seems to be the topic, which sparks many concerns and fears as you wonder who will measure up. Examples of morality are at an all time low, when church members are jeopardizing your salvation outside of the "Sanctuary." Considering the fact that Christians should be an example of a changed mind and lifestyle, but they act superior and full of deceit. Those same Christians seldom fellowship outside of the churches; and make indecent proposals between the sheets.

It's gotten to the point that people don't have time to share Jesus unless being prompted by someone else to get motivated and get involved. Very seldom people genuinely offer to help someone else in need, without looking for some gratuity or act of being noticed. My thoughts are to strive to be the best I can be, because the Bible states clearly that "No not one" will be without sin. Love God with all thy heart and soul and thy neighbor as thy self. Never forget however, that Satan is busy. Do your best to share the compassion of your heart, planting seeds of encouragement one life at a time, until fruition.

Then when things get really tough and the end of days is upon us, kneel and pray. When you put God first then all things are possible and added unto you. We all have fallen short of the glory of God! Stop beating yourself up because of your past or what you did five minutes ago because Jesus can fix it. You'll have peace knowing that Jesus came to save and not to destroy. Stay encouraged during the perilous times among us.

Trapped In a Maze of Drugs

Clothes wrinkled, hair a mess, I don't know my direction from east or west. Looking for a place to lay my head, all is lost I wish I was dead. My last dime was towards chasing a high; I sold my body just to get by.

Crack cocaine and even ice, whether I lived through the day was a roll of the dice. I can't be trusted wherever I go. I'll steal from you to secure me some blow, snorting drugs up my nose, or tying off my veins with a thin rubber hose. Going to rehab and not having any luck, because the real reason was "I didn't give a fuck".

My reality is not usually the same; it's a vicious cycle of me being insane. I promise when I'm sober and broke that I won't do any drugs, or even smoke.

I'll lie through my teeth just to get what I want, continuing in drugs as I go on the hunt. Hanging out with addicts and begging for a fix, consuming any drug, while making myself sick. My teeth have turned yellow and I don't own a brush, I'm not even desirable and I don't feel any lust.

I'm scrounging around on the streets as I walk, picking up anything and to myself I do talk. I'm caught in a maze of drug filled madness, cursing you because I have this addictive sadness.

So my advice if I had some to give, don't enable a junkie if you want them to live.

Letting Go

You want me to let go, but how can I? I remember your smell, your touch, your breath upon my cheek, and your tongue softly licking my ear lobes. I close my eyes as I inhale your essence around me. I can't let go; the memories are too fresh in my mind.

This once happy couple has crumpled into a mess of sad memories and regrets. Everywhere I turn I see you, in the faces of others, thinking about the excitement of the precious moments shared, when I knew I was your prize. The security of your protective nature no longer comfort me, as I realized just how good you were for me.

I cry out in the night your name, but I'm stuck in a veil of silence. Feels like I'm suspended in air gasping for each breath that I take. I drown in a whirlwind of memories and tears as my mind spins out of control.

My flesh and my heart flutter within me, bringing me back to reality, with a vibrating pulsation of electrical impulses that travel from my fingertips to my chest with each nervous moment that passes before me.

Just remembering creates torture to my soul, now I'm stretched out here on the doctor's bench having a

GYN inspection, not sure of whether I'm pregnant or not but with my eyes closed the touch seems so familiar upon my thighs.

This is only a check-up, and I can't get you off of my mind, how you have always been there for me, reassuring and comforting. This is one of the many precious moments which I remember. So how can I let go?

Don't You Feel Stupid?

Don't say that you never felt stupid and here's why. Remember the time you yelled, cursed, and hurt someone else's feelings because you thought they said something behind your back, but you found out later that they didn't? It should have made you feel stupid.
Don't you feel stupid when the person of your affection has just used you for your body and devotion, while cheating on you behind your back, was that a dumb move or do you feel stupid?
Don't you feel stupid when you find out that you threw away a letter that contained a check that you could have used because you were flat broke and busted; now you need some money and no one can help you?
Don't you feel stupid the first time you rush out of the house to run a quick errand while you're looking a hot mess and some attractive person that you admire happens to look your way, and you can't duck fast enough?
Don't you feel stupid when you fail a test that you thought was easy because you were too lazy to study, and you have to wait a long time for a make-up test?
Don't you feel stupid when you're out in public, your stomach is rumbling, you pick a bathroom

stall without any toilet paper; you have to go
real bad and there's a line forming for the next
available stall and you have to yell for assistance?
Don't you feel stupid when you sneeze and mucus
comes out of your nose and you have no tissue handy
and everyone is watching for your next move?
Don't you feel stupid when you load up your
shopping cart and when you get to the counter
you don't have you wallet with you?
Don't you feel stupid when you're trying to act
cute, when all of a sudden you trip and fall down?
So you lay there and play hurt because everyone's
watching and no one offers to help you up.

Don't you feel stupid sometimes when you
think you are acting intelligent, and everything
that comes out of your mouth sounds dumb;
you make up words to fit the scenario and
everyone is laughing and staring at you?
Don't you feel stupid sometimes when
someone asks you for your phone
number and your brain goes blank?
Don't you feel stupid sometimes for getting mad
at someone about something you dreamt and you
didn't even realize it was a dream, and you're
fussing and everyone is staring at you in awe?
Don't you feel stupid sometimes just because
we all have a hidden touch of madness waiting
to pop up at the wrong time and it usually picks

the moment you're trying to be cultured? Isn't it wonderful to play stupid but not be stupid, because stupid is as stupid does.

Bad Odors

Some people have bad odors and
some people don't care.
Some have bad odors, and the smell is in their hair.
Some people have bad odors because
they hate to brush their teeth.
The smell is so nasty and it smells like rotting beef.

Some people have bad odors from
the smell of cigarette smoke.
The smell is so horrible it will make you choke.
Some people have bad odors because
they over do everything.
People are consuming so much garlic
to keep their system clean.

Some people have bad odors because
they hardly take a bath,
washing their body in the sink
when they should be soaking their ass.

Some people have bad odors because
their clothes, they won't change.
They wear the same clothes over and
over, even with the stains.
Some people have bad odors from

the medicines that they take.
It seeps through their pores; this
problem they cannot fake.

Some people have bad odors because
they drink too much.
The smell will cling to them and
everything they touch.
Some people have bad odors
because they play in the dirt.
But when it's kids that smell, it doesn't really hurt?

You Don't Know Me

You don't know me and I don't know you, I'm the female that you tried to abuse. Breaking my phone and gluing my door, I couldn't open it from inside anymore.

I was two floors up, and I had to escape, so I jumped from my balcony into the bushes that waited, and I was bruised all over. This choice I hated, but I had to do it if I was to make it. I was pricked from the thorns of the bush, with leaves in my hair and I ran like whoosh.

I ran to my car and I was shocked to see, neither steering wheel, nor a door lock for a key. I had to think, "What next should I do?" I hid behind some bushes and was afraid to move. When he got back and went towards the house, I ran the opposite way, quiet as a mouse.

I flagged down a taxi and jumped in real quick, my stomach was bubbling and when inside, I felt sick. I was taken to a hotel and then I called the police, looking forward to one night sleeping in peace. I vowed that day that he would suffer, because he didn't know me, that crazy old buzzard.

I pressed charges and I made sure they would stick, because I had had enough of his dumb ass shit. You don't know me, but one thing is true, I'm not going to live this nightmare over, not even for you.

Man Trouble

Know when to heed the warning signs.
It's not ok to be disrespected.
It's not ok to be hit.
It's not ok to be frightened, because
you and your mate don't agree.
It's not ok to be used as a sex slave
when you have said no.
It's not ok to be a prisoner in your home.
It's not ok to be unable to make your own choices.
It's not ok to be unable to spend your own paycheck.
It's not ok for your eyes to be puffy
from crying each day.
It's not ok to be hurt and have no one to turn to.
It's not ok to stay afraid….If he
makes you feel this way,
then you have man trouble. Seek Help immediately.

TERRY LYLE

If Walls Could Talk

If walls could talk, what would they reveal?
Would it tell your story of how you lie and steal?
If walls could talk, what would they see,
another person in your bed other than me?
If walls could talk would you be ashamed?
Your name would be tarnished,
with your perverted sex games.
If walls could talk,
what would you hide,
Your junkie, filthy home
with roaches inside?
If walls could talk, what would they say,
You steal money from your job and hide it away?
If walls could talk, what would they hear
the screams of those living in fear?
If walls could talk, what story could be told,
wrinkled old people,
not wearing any clothes?
If walls could talk,
what's the worst they could say,
your tub is dirty and you don't even bathe?
If walls could talk,
what would they say about you,
you're constantly medicated and paranoid too?
If walls could talk,

would they make a frown?
because you've been exposed,
as a cross dressing clown?
If walls could talk,
what would they whisper about you?
Would they tell you were molested
around the age of two?
If walls could talk, would they be happy or sad or,
would they shake their head, recalling
the life that you had?

TERRY LYLE

Nina And Derrick

Once upon a time, a long time ago
Nina met Derrick
and their story is told
about
two lovers who now became one.
He's the moon and she's his sun.
Like anyone else
they had their ups and their downs
but love overruled and Nina's still around.
It wasn't love at first sight
she just happened to be
that special love he needed to see.
She's a fine woman and he's a handsome guy
he winked at her as she walked by.
The spark grew deeper a little over time,
now it's a raging fire and their love is just fine.
Lovingly walking through their life,
you'll find Coach Derrick and Nina his wife.

That's What You Said

How many times have you told me that you were coming over, but you didn't show? You became frustrated with me because I became irritated, but isn't that what you said?
You think I'm holding on too tight because I hold you responsible for your words, expecting accountability and action, but when I complain you point your finger at me and say I have a problem, but aren't we talking about what you said?
It's no wonder I have a problem putting my faith and trust back into you. Whenever you fall short or lack follow through, it's me you seem to think who doesn't understand because I just respond to something that you said.
Every time this occurs, I look over my life and wonder am I fooling myself, if the small accountability issues can't be made, then how can I trust my spirit to the larger issues?
You would like to make your flaws appear to be so trivial and my disappointments minor, but really, "Life will go on with or without you." I'm listening real hard and watching for the things that you say and when I'm fed up with you, I'll be on my way. I'm tired of mimicking "That's what you said."

TERRY LYLE

Road Rage

Driving in my car and feeling fine, when I felt a thump on my car's behind. I turned around and what did I see? I saw an angry tall man walking towards me. All of a sudden he was grabbing on my door. I yelled, "Hold up sucker I'm not going to take much more."
He was cursing and screaming and flipping out, so I jumped on my cell phone without a doubt. I was mad when I picked up my phone; I called for backup from my brothers at home. This man was complaining that I had cut him off; I stared at him like his brain was soft.
He had road rage and was in my face, so I rolled up my window quickly, in haste. I couldn't leave because he had hit my car and I was staying until the problem was resolved. Shortly afterwards came my brothers and they whipped on him like they were his mother. Arms were swinging all over the place, this fight pursued because of road rage. Things turned from bad to worse after the police arrived and made a search. Checking out the vehicle and looking for weapons because things had escalated from what had just happened.
I'm not the one who usually gets mad, but that

buster had road rage really bad. Everyone was taken to the police station, and I needed a drink, I needed libation. Hours later I had a chance to go home, pissed off about road rage all night long.

Sliding On Thin Ice

You're skating on thin ice but I'm not talking about in a rink. I'm talking about your attitude, the way you relate to people stinks. You've been blessed to have a lot of things and why are you flashing all of your bling?

Have you heard that old wise tale that, "You meet the same people going up as you do going down?" How far will you drop if your friends aren't around?

I've constantly warned you, I can't take it anymore; I want you to act more normal instead of being a bore. Show some interest in someone other than yourself and get off your "Me, Me, Me, ice block" before it melts.

If the truth be told you didn't start off with much, remember sliding on thin ice while flagging down a bus. Your clothes were brought off the $5.00 rack, now you're wearing tailored stuff on your back.

You have gotten so full of yourself and someone needs to tell you, before anything else, stop slipping away because you're sliding on thin ice today. If you haven't saved any money yet, then you will have some big regrets. Try to figure out a different way to show happiness without going astray. Be gracious when you entertain and try to be nice and not act insane.

The one, who has financed you, has finally given up, because your attitude stinks and your attitude sucks. So I'm trying to warn you to change your views. The buzz that's going around is that you're going to lose, all of your precious things real soon.

Your man has warned you since you have started sliding on thin ice, but you never listen, not even twice. I'm trying to bless you with some knowledge that I have; you can listen or you can laugh. Sweetie the bus stops are crowded still, even wearing your prettiest heels.

I've known you all of your life; you started changing when there was no ice. The ice of struggles and making it on your own, but now you're complacent in your big fancy home. Well one day soon we'll meet again, when every thing's gone and you need a friend.

Raped

I'm snatched into an alley by some unknown figure, beaten and raped and my body shivers while shaking uncontrollable, and my screams went unheard inside my brain, this was totally absurd. My innocence was taken and I'll suffer mental scars, the pain runs so deep I'm left with no trust at all. Why was I chosen to become a victim of rape? Why couldn't I find any exits of escape? I'm afraid and withdrawn and I don't go out at night; no longer happy go lucky and I trust no one by sight. I'm filled with terror every day with screams in my head that won't go away. No longer will I suffer this pain anymore, I've found a conclusion that can't be ignored. My life has changed and I don't like it as much, I need to forget about suicide because that option is out. I don't want to kill myself because the pain won't go away; I refuse to be raped in my mind each day. Stand with me as together we pray that one day soon, this pain goes away.

Forgiveness

Forgiveness sometimes in your life
may seem to be the hardest thing to do.
I think about the times when
I've been personally victimized and
it's hard to let go of that negative feeling.

I realize that I'm far from perfect
I'm sure there are more mountains
to climb, rivers to cross,
and hurdles to jump over.
I'm sure that somewhere in life
I will need forgiveness

Forgiveness has to start with me
The Bible clearly states that,
"If you can't forgive,
then why should God forgive you?
I love the Lord
and I'll never be perfect
because it has already been prophesied.

I want to see Jesus
and the rest of my family that made it to
Heaven.
I won't let go of my faith,

TERRY LYLE

so I will learn to forgive
and move on in my life
without the bitterness of my past
holding me captive
because,
Where would I be if God didn't forgive me?

You

When I think of you many things flood my mind, your smile, your touch, and the sparkle in your eyes when you're happy. I wonder will I see that again because the wall between us has grown invisible, it appears, yet the restraint of letting our guard down is so obvious.

Many times on this merry-go-round of emotions I wondered who would still be there for me in a moment's notice and I see your face reassuring me that all is well. I try to remember the last time you and I were in perfect harmony and the turning point that our relationship started to decay. I toss and turn when I think of what I should do next?

As I awake from this dream of discomfort, I realize that what I thought was you turned out really to be me staring back at me, always that quiet hope of surviving a broken heart because loneliness has become my friend. Were you my life preserver or an illusion in my head?

Racism Madness

When you're tired of racism and someone tells you life is just the cards you've been dealt, don't complain and suck it up while never knowing what it's like to be a victim of racism. You should continue standing proud with dignity, integrity and hope for change in the future, as you overcame your past moving forward to enlighten the youth of today through words of wisdom.

There are many types of cards that we choose to play, but dealing with life with racism just isn't the way. Racism isn't pretty and it's very unkind, you shatter and humiliate when you put others down.

Why can't we live together like unified brothers? Let's fight for equality one for the other. This way we all may gain, instead of hurting each other, which is really a shame. That's dumb that old racism game, how can abuse of another bring profit or gain?

So what if your eyes are blue and mine are brown, we still find discouragement to be profound. We struggle daily to provide for our kids, with hope of maintaining shelter, food and a bed. We all have loved and even have lost, but we continue daily no matter the cost.

We live in a world where difference is the key to unlocking many beautiful unknown mysteries. Embrace humanity with love and respect, while putting the racism madness completely in check.

Secrets

Secrets are thoughts that you share.
Secrets can be controversial, a leak you cannot bear.
Secrets are things whispered between friends.
Even though visually, you look like cackling hens.

It's a must that secrets be shared
with people you trust.
If secrets are issues that will make you fuss,
then
they are the same issues that will make you cuss.

Secrets can be explosive or secrets can be nice.
The secret could be hiding the time,
you plan to propose to your wife.

A secret could be planning a private affair,
for a special guest to share.
A secret is working undercover
without the knowledge of the general public.

Secrets are private and secluded,
and
known only to few.
Could you hold a secret if I shared one with you?

Growing Up

I remember when I was growing up; I constantly heard the words, "Why don't you shut up."

My mouth would be running a mile a minute, that's how it was in the beginning.

They would say that kids were seen and not heard, so you learned what conversations not to disturb.

Electrical cords, switches, and sticks, are things that were used when we used to get hit.

We seemed to be more respectful back then, not living a life that's full of sin.

Our manners were easy to see, "yes sir, no ma'am, thank you, and please."

Today things are different and it's really sad, people don't appreciate what blessings they have.

Back in the day, as I remembered, my favorite holiday was in December.

Waiting to receive the gifts under the tree, we were lucky if we got more than three.

Sometimes breakfast was biscuits and syrup, and hot tea that we would slurp.

Going to the movie didn't cost much, and candy was cheap, even riding the bus.

TERRY LYLE

Now today the same values we used to have are wonderful memories of our past.

Growing up back then wasn't so bad; it taught us how to be happy for what we had.

You Tell Me You Love Me

You tell me you love me, and I'll say you're a liar.
You tell me you love me until the day that you die.
You tell me you love me, yet you
quickly slipped away.
Secretly into the arms of another,
you left me crying that day.
You tell me you love me are the words that I hear.
Inside my heart is dismayed, that feeling is real.
The pain is intense, I got a raw deal.
You tell me you love me like I love you,
but I'm still here waiting and there's no sign of you.
You tell me you love me and I'm left all alone.
You need to come back, you need to come home.

TERRY LYLE

Being a Victim

The day went extremely well, I was out visiting with family and friends.

It was getting late and the night was approaching fast. I was asked to give a ride to some friends, who hopped into my car. Also along for the ride came my little grandson.

We were only into ten minutes of our trip, when I looked down the road and saw mattresses and garbage blocking most of the roadway. I slowed down to maneuver around those items, when out of nowhere several youth appeared with guns in our faces.

They began to yell for us to get out of the car. Fearing we would die right there, I started to fight back. I wrestled with the guy with the gun closest to me through my car window.

Successfully I was able to pull the gun from his grip and started shooting in his direction while speeding off.

Losing all sense of direction, I found myself in a situation worse than the one before. We ended up on a deserted dead end street with decaying buildings all around us.

Shocked and frightened as we all were, I turned around, so that I could back out of this street. That's when I saw a menacing crowd of gang bangers. As they surrounded my car, I knew there were no means of escape.

One by one we were snatched out of the vehicle. I cried and pleaded and reached for my grandson but he disappeared into the crowd. The other two females were taken and from the corner of my eye, I saw them being brutally raped and sodomized.

My torture I suppose would come later, because the guy whose gun I took earlier said, "Leave her for me." He smacked me in my face and grabbed me by my throat. He then led me away into one of the abandoned buildings. Inside horrified, and not knowing what would happen next, I glanced around looking for options.

Slowly he began unzipping his pants, while telling me what he planned to do to me. As he stood before me, some more of his friends came in and the noise distraction made him turn around. I used that opportunity to kick him in the groin and I ran like a mad man, deeper into this building, looking for a hiding place.

I could hear voices all around me saying to come out. I made it to the lower levels of this building, which was filled with broken pieces of furniture, rats, and trash everywhere. In desperation I saw hope, there was a wooden door that might lead me out of here.

Sweating profusely and turning around, afraid to be recaptured, I pulled violently on the door and it swung open, with what appeared to be a blinding light. Peaceful it seemed at that instant, but it became dark once again and I ran. My heart violently beating in my chest, I ran without turning back.

Eventually I saw stores and businesses and people going about their lives. I ran into a store seeking help. When I noticed some friends of mine there and I recounted my previous experience with them. With renewed hope it was time to get the police, find my grandson and friends who were in my car.

In the flurry of confusion and on lookers, I looked around for any signs of my attackers. Giving every detail I could, ok I yelled for them to speed up the process and start the search.

With extreme anguish I watched as time ticked by without any revealing news. I feared the worst because I knew I was still a victim.

Advice For Young Ladies Dating

When you're young and think you're in love and the question of sex comes up, don't hesitate because this is what you need to do. First grab your things and head for the door, say no and if he respects you, he'll let you go. He might say let's have some fun, but my advice to you is:

RUN,RUN, RUN!

Get your education first before the choices you make in life turn out worst. Having a baby when you're young is a responsibility that can't be undone; it's a sad outcome to little boys saying let's have fun. Here's a hint: if he can't take care of himself, then having sex with him doesn't make any sense. It's not someone else's responsibility to raise your child because of your choices and living wild. "Don't be dumb, and don't forget the key word isn't cum, but the key word is run"!!!

TERRY LYLE

Distracted

I'm distracted by your light and I'm
drawn towards your face.
I'm distracted by your handsomeness,
as I hug you around your waist.
I'm distracted by your body; "it's
so tight and oh so fine".
I'm distracted by your smile because
it lets me know you're mine.
I'm distracted by your eyes and
the contacts that you wear.
I'm distracted by the color that's
always changing of your hair.
I'm distracted by the way you dress
because you truly have some flair.
I'm distracted by our lovemaking; I can't
get enough when you are here. Sometimes
it even makes me lose my mind.
With random thoughts running through my head.
I'm distracted by the mirrors, as
I check out your behind.
I'm distracted by your smell as
your scent it draws me near.
I'm distracted by so many things
because I'm medicated this year.

Yelling Into The Silence

Your life is filled with turmoil that you feel as though
you're yelling into your silence.
The pressures of life have you in a bind,
all that is replaced is bitterness and
you need to explode,
but
you start yelling into the silence.
Days have lingered on into months.
Nothing is going right.
Drama is unfolding all around you
to find relief.
You start yelling into the silence.
It's late in the midnight hour,
no sounds can be heard,
but your brain overloads
you can't imagine what's going on.
In your mind
you feel frantic
when you start yelling into the silence.

TERRY LYLE

Inspiration

Inspiration comes from many sources but my main source is from God. Often I find a special person that will inspire me to do my best and I want to do so, hoping that they will be pleased.

Family is also an area from which to draw for your inspiration, watching their cheerful outlook on life and the positivity that glows around them.

Children are always a source of inspiration, just because they depend on you for support, love, and protection, while the responsibility inside you churns to never let them down.

Inspiration can come from witnessing the kind deeds of others towards another, that it grabs your heart and make your eyes burn, while holding back tears of warm sentiment.

Inspiration sometimes comes from witnessing the courage under fire of our patriotic men and women fighting and dying for the safety of our nation, while keeping terrorism away from the home front; proudly wearing the colors of our military branches.

Inspiration comes from listening to testimonies of others in near death experiences, knowing you couldn't survive what they went through, and too insecure to display the scars of the aftermath where all can see.

Alone

Alone again! Sitting here waiting for you to show, the phone doesn't ring and you're trying to be optimistic. Inside you're hurt, angry, deeply shattered, and unable to speak. You painstakingly refuse to let any emotions show through your eyes because of the rage boiling inside of you.

It's imperative that your emotions be protected and concealed at all costs, so they don't suffer the decay of a breakdown in understanding; judging not and afraid to allow any break down from the outside of your understanding because that's all you have to cling to. When they don't understand, then there are emotional outbursts and excuses for their behavior. Yet you're penalized because you verbalize the unfairness of their behavior.

You don't care for me like I thought you did or I wouldn't be feeling this low; and you let me slip further into that dark, sinister place of anger, frustration, and despair. Your selfishness has hit an all time low. It's always about you and why you think I need to get over it when you're not accountable. It's always supposed to be ok if my time is ruined while waiting on you and I'm stuck alone when I had choices that I turned down.

I find myself turning aimlessly around looking for means of escape, trapped in the dementia of my mind with quiet silence prickling my neck, breathing cautiously as I realize that I'm alone.

Watch Out

Watch out I'm coming for you
as I hide in the darkness
concealed from your view.
Watch out if you have a dollar,
I'll take your money and make you holler.
Watch out I'm waiting for you,
to mug you is the thing that I'll do.
Watch out because I'm a creature of the night.
I will murder you before it gets light.
Watch out and look left and look right.
I'm
craving the blood that I will spill tonight.
Watch out and stay on alert.
Police can't save you
when I come out to work.
Watch out because evil is me,
I have mercy for none that I see.
Watch out because evil will feed
and flourish like strong,
overgrown weeds
Watch out!!!

TERRY LYLE

Pregnancy

Pregnant and you're the only one that knows; scared and excited by the new life growing inside of you, yet confused about whether you can provide for a child.

As a teenager, getting pregnant and scared to tell your parents, you may sometimes think of ways to kill the child inside of you that is growing, while endangering your own life with foreign objects to induce miscarriages.

Young married couples struggle, trying hard to make ends meet, immediately becoming discouraged when up pops another pregnancy. Or maybe it's your first one and you're living from day to day in constant despair, barely able to feed yourself, let alone another life, wondering what should be done next.

You're away at college having the time of your life, getting good grades and you slip up and go to a party and leave your drink unattended. You wake up ashamed and a victim of date rape. Now you're pregnant and don't know who the father is and afraid to share your stupidity from your bad choices.

Middle aged and comfortable with grown children, you enjoy the stability and contentment in your life. Fast approaching menopause, when out of the blue, you realize that stomach ache you had was morning sickness. You thought your baby making days were behind you, but now they are once again smacking you in the face.

You have a history of female problems and would love to become a parent, but you were told you couldn't have children. Then you find yourself in an unexpected pregnancy because you didn't take precautions; but now it's an ectopic pregnancy and the odds are stacked against you.

You're an offspring of very strict parents that you're afraid to disappoint, or you had no options against becoming a mom, because someone took advantage of you. With a fleeting glimmer of wishful thinking, you think of how wonderful it would feel to be a mom, having someone love you and accept your shortcomings.

Life is growing inside of you that you want to hate because the dad refuses to take the new packaged deal, or maybe your dad is your baby's dad too, because you've been a victim of incest.

Financially ready and able to have a child, you do everything right in the prenatal stages and while on a visit to the doctor's office, you're told there are some abnormalities to the pregnancy and maybe you will need to abort.

Pregnancy means a lot of things to different people, but giving life is always a special achievement and blessing.

Giddy

Heck yeah I'm giddy
I'm the girl they call real pretty;
standing here in my gown,
representing my hometown.
I'm trying to win the beauty crown
to show young girls that dreams are found.
Now it's time for the talent show,
I hope I place really close.
Even though I won't try to boast,
it seems I'm the favorite beauty
they love the most.
I'm still giddy standing here beside the host.
Excitement beams all over my face
knowing my prep work didn't go to waste.
Heck yeah I'm happy and giddy too
standing here sweating
and
shaking in my shoes.
Here comes the moment now
I want to win that pretty crown.

TERRY LYLE

Website Friends

I would like to become a friend on this website, where should I begin? I haven't earned any money and some think that's funny.

I've busted my rump writing articles through the night, just to see that my earnings haven't increased, knowing that ain't right.

When you're new to a website it isn't much fun, you'll look around and notice the same spot where you begun.

Shucks I haven't made any money since I have been here; I've earned only a penny unfortunately this year. I'm so full of fear that my stuff you won't like, I tweak it over and over trying to make it just right.

I would appreciate any offer of advice you may have, so my earnings won't always come up last. But if you choose not to give it to me, then I'll have to live with your empathy.

I think that I will continue to explore different types of money options, which I won't ignore. I read everyone's articles and I put in a lot of time on multiple websites so I'll be fine.

There are Triond, Redgage, and Lulu too. There are several, actually, quite a few. For me it seems truly a waste of my time I'm still writing while trying to earn a dime.

My goal is to make some money this year, and if a penny is it, then I need to stop right here. I don't know anyone who has received a large pay, however the writers will continue anyway, some will write for exposure, and possible fame, but when I write it's for personal gain.

That's The Way It Is

I'm not going to play the fool because you're my boo.
It's a term I lovingly use when I think about you,
and that's the way it is.
I don't want your man, I just need a financial hand,
and that's the way it is.
I'll steal some of his time while I dance on his mind,
and that's the way it is.
Where he's at is where he wants to be,
you need to deal with him and not with me,
and that's the way it is.
Don't make your issues about me
because you aren't being treated
the way you want to be,
and that's the way is
All those sexual tricks that you're starting to enjoy,
he learned them from me. I showed him the score
and that's the way it is.
So before you start tripping,
It's his fault
that
he's over here dipping,
and that's the way it is

Moochers

I don't know why I allowed you to stay in my home,
I wish right now that you were gone.
You never offer to pay any rent
while you hang around when your money is spent.
In front of the television when you're in the house,
you won't do any work because you're a louse.
This is a big part of your attitude that stinks,
you won't even wash any dishes that's in the sink.
You must think that because I care for you,
it's ok to treat me like your fool.
You act like you're allergic to a broom,
get off your butt and clean the room.
Cooking food that's not your own,
those are groceries that I brought home.
I go to work and you stay home,
something about this picture is definitely wrong.
Lazy you are with a capital L,
but
I'm tired of this stuff you can go to hell.

TERRY LYLE

I Can't Wait To See You

Baby here I am
sitting on a cloud
Waiting on you to stop on by
You're my lover,
my friend, and so much more,
I'm looking forward to you
walking through my door.
As I stare at your picture
and glance at your smile,
your numbers I'm really tempted to dial.
I get so excited
thinking
about the next time you'll be here with me,
as you caress and touch my body.
I haven't lost sight of my dreams,
"Oh no not by any means,"
but
I can't wait to see you.

Cute

Don't get mad because I'm cute,
yes my horn I like to toot.
Try to enjoy what you have,
because all beauty doesn't last.
If your beauty is only skin deep,
what will happen
when you're a wrinkled heap?
One day I'll get older and I'll wrinkle quick,
then my beauty won't mean a lick.
Unless it's internal and shines throughout
then otherwise, I'll just be a wrinkled old mouth.
It's true, that beauty on the outside
is a temporary thing,
as real beauty will start from within.
Being a kind and gentle soul
is the type of beauty
that will break the mold.
So don't worry if someone thinks you're cute
because your horn you like to toot.
Continue to be the person that you are
because in someone's eyes
"You're still a star."

TERRY LYLE

Two Souls

Boldly I step towards you
trusting our love is true.
You're here to love me
as I'll love you back
Together we're perfectly matched.
From my heart to yours
I'll give you my soul.
Take it and watch my love unfold.
Precious you are and always will be,
as you've given always your best to me.
I can't express what you mean to my life,
but without you I couldn't suffice.
As my heart beats
each minute of the day,
my love grows stronger in every way.
I'm so glad we're perfectly matched,
two souls that are still attached.

I Give Up

Constant disagreements take you to your breaking point. You have lost the ability to listen to your lover's heart. Harsh words said in anger so quickly depart from the same lips that together, in tenderness was taught, on many occasions, when you confessed your heart. Painfully you hurt the other, usually one will be strong and the other one will blubber. Their tears may not always show on the outside, they hold them within because of their pride. You've come to your crossroads of understanding and afraid to be honest when you should give up; inside there's turmoil that really sucks. Constantly you hold on to the dreams of your past, looking toward to your future, and thinking. "Can this relationship last?" Saying I give up isn't the easiest thing to do, but sometimes you need to be true to your heart and do what is best for you.
"I give up and I'm releasing you".

Respect

Everyone needs to practice respect
especially if they want it back.
Talk is cheap and your words are sweet
but respect is something I want to keep.
I will respect you and you should respect me,
I'll treat you like a human should
be treated most respectfully.
Respect was taught by my mom and my dad,
one of the qualities that they had.
They did their best while raising us kids,
never reneging on what they placed in our heads.
I remember many other qualities as well,
those are the stories that I tell.
I'm so glad that I learned respect,
It's needed in life on every step.
It's said that what goes in
will definitely come out,
hopefully respect
will be
what
I'm known about.

Church

I'm going to church as soon as I can
as I wait for the driver with the van.
They will pick me up
and take me on my way,
to the house of worship
where I want to pray.
I'll fellowship with the people
who are worshipping there,
my story about Jesus
I'm willing to share.
I truly have
a real testimony
about how Jesus
never left me
lost or lonely.
So I'm sitting here
waiting on the van
to escort me to church,
that is my plan.
To get me there as soon as I can.

TERRY LYLE

Somebody Told You Wrong

Somebody must have told you wrong. You need to
check yourself, you need to step back, because your
ideas are totally whack. Screaming and fussing
doesn't work on me and your face I don't want to see.
So you need to get off my back and
I'm not trying to hear your flak.
What makes you think that I have to jump when
you call? With that attitude you're doomed
to fall, flat on your face with no help in sight,
because all you do is argue and fight?
No one is trying to hear this mess every day about
how things aren't going your way. To hear you tell it
everyone is wrong, you sing that same tired old song.
You're always the first to ask for help, but you
do it while you holler and yelp. Locked up and
want someone to answer your calls, you're so
irritable they aren't trying to hear you at all.
You always have some crucial demands,
expecting others to jump to it,
because
of what you're saying.
Everyone has a life that they need to attend to,
so stop acting like they should focus on you.
Everything you want you expect to have first,

and the way you sound comes off like a jerk.
Somebody must have told you wrong; you first
need to learn what it takes to get along.
At times when you even offer some help,
I'll wind up hearing about it from someone
else. You've created so much stress; that
everyone's tired of hearing your mess.

APPENDIX A *

(Awesome collection of works by aspiring amateur poets and writers whose permission was granted to be showcased here without monetary rewards.)

- A-1 Where were you when God called you? by Sylvia L.Robertson, Baltimore, MD
- A-2 The day I meet my true love by Mary Glaspole, The United Kingdom, England
- A-3 I have nothing to say by Carol "Lucille" Robertson, Brooklyn, NY
- A-4 It's about time by Karen R. Robertson, Brooklyn, NY
- A-5 Hands by Lola M. Matthews, Laurens, SC
- A-6 Woman… (You bought me up) by Mykeal Eternal the Poet Crapper, Baltimore, MD
- A-7 I am not African; I am something else (A letter to the so called "real" African American) by Mykeal Eternal the Poet Crapper, Baltimore, MD
- A-8 You bring joy to me by Karlis N. Wright, New York/Montgomery, AL

A-9 Have I ever been in love? By Karlis N. Wright, New York/Montgomery, Alabama

A-10 Feelings of the Tell, Tell, Heart by Karlis N. Wright, New York/Montgomery, Alabama

A-11 For the sake of love by Samuel Alexander, St. Vincent, Caribbean/ Opelika, Alabama

A-12 Jesus is Knocking by Jeffrey L. Duke, Cincinnati, Ohio

A-13 The Fight by Jim Swettenham, Winnipeg, Manitoba, Canada

A-14 Hurt Pride by Jim Swettenham, Winnipeg, Manitoba, Canada

A-15 Menopause Meanies by Jim Swettenham, Winnipeg, Manitoba, Canada

A-16 Exercise your Funny Bone/The bride and the Groom by Marlene Ramirez-Journalist, Sunshine State of Florida

A-17 Bikini Lines by Marlene Ramirez-journalist, Sunshine State of Florida

A-18 Warrior Creed by Obikelvin, Limbe Cameroon, Africa

A-19 Giving a Damn by Obikelvin, Limbe Cameroon, Africa

A-20 Never Leave me Angry/Quench by Neva Flores, Columbus, GA

A-21 You Just Can't by Lovely Honey, Montreal, Canada

A-22 Black Cracker Baseball by Tracy Duke Arnold, Columbus, Georgia

Where were you when God called you?

Sylvia L. Robertson
Baltimore, Maryland

Were you like me, alone in my bed, sleeping
quite peacefully, dreams in my head?
I suddenly sat up, fear taking control, shaking
like crazy. Was it really that cold?
I heard it quite clearly, someone calling my name. I
glanced around nervously, thinking I was insane.
I couldn't decide just what I should do. Was
I losing my mind? No, that can't be true.
I swung my legs over the side of the bed. To
tell you the truth, hell yeah I was scared.
I reached for the light switch, I wanted to see. Was
it my imagination or someone messing with me?
The light seemed so dim, I still wasn't sure. Could
it be possible, was that a knock at the door?
With my heart in my throat, I was ready to run.
I was mad at myself for not having a gun.
I peeked through the peep hole, there
was nothing to see; Only a grey cloud
of smoke inching closer to me.
I opened the door, what else could I do? Maybe

TERRY LYLE

I was just stupid. I thought of that too.
Suddenly my senses started to take hold, warning
me that something was out of control.
The smell was so acrid, the heat so intense. It
was time to get out if I had any sense.

I raced down the stairway, yelling quite loud,
fighting my way through an enveloping cloud.
Watching my neighbors as they ran out the door,
hoping and praying that there weren't any more.
Much later on when peace was restored, it
finally dawned on me that it was the **LORD**
Despite my transgression and wrongs I had done,
He stayed there beside me for He is the one.
To protect me and guide me wherever I roam.
I finally realized it was time to go home.
Back to the one place where love is so true. So
tell me, where were you when God called you?

The day I met my True Love

Mary Glaspole
United Kingdom

The day I meet my true love
will be the day
I haven't washed my hair
for a week.

The one time I skip
brushing my teeth
forget my deodorant
and my razor misses
some hairs behind my knee.

The day I meet my true love
there will be snow,
I'll have icicles on my lashes,
dripping mascara patches
and bright pink cheeks.
Windswept looking,
tangled, I will arrive.

TERRY LYLE

The day I meet my true love
the til will freeze
with my dinner and wine on the conveyor
anticipating bagging.
The checkout girl will look at me vacantly
"I will have to call the manager"
she will wander off.
It's raining.

The day I meet my true love
I will have gotten stuck in a meeting
and had trouble with my brakes.
Putting my hood up to hide
I will pray I have time
to bathe

but reading the number plate at twenty feet
he is early.
And when we've met and eaten out,
laughed through a movie
and over drinks
I'll see his face book relationship status.

I Have Nothing to Say

Carol "Lucille" Robertson
Brooklyn, New York

I have nothing to say.
I don't want any part of your drama.
Don't ask me any questions.
"Don't you see I'm here resting"?
I'm not that kind of woman.
And I have nothing to say,
So you can leave right now,
And go on your way
Didn't you hear what I said?
"I have nothing to say".

It's about Time

Karen R. Robertson
Brooklyn, New York

It's about time that, I move out on my own.
I need my own space now that I'm grown.
I need the room so I can have some fun,
Dropping it like it's hot, until the morning sun.
It's about time that I start a new life,
While being cautious and packing a knife.
Looking forward, towards adventures unknown,
This is what I'll do, now that I am grown.

Hands

Lola M. Matthews
Laurens, South Carolina

It's all about love, but not considered work
That's why I'm a happy,
Greeter at church
With arms outstretched,
with my hands open wide
A flow of people are coming in tides
Lovingly embracing you
the way that I do,
Is how I show my love's sincere and true,
When I'm thinking about the LORD
I have outstretched hands, and I am thanking him
for his master's plan.
He gives me love sincere and true,
it flows from his heart, through my hands to you.
I use my hands to touch
hug and embrace a child,
just so I, could see their smiles.
With God's hands on my life,
out comes the qualities that are nice.
When you think of GOD'S love
you'll have to smile,
knowing Jesus will return in a little while.

TERRY LYLE

Woman

"You brought me up"
Makeal, Eternal the Poet Crapper
Columbus, Georgia

You brought me up
Set my feet atop mountains
So I could look across the ocean
and see what part of the earth I would conquer next.
With blood, sweat, and tears
You…brought me up.
Rivers of blood flooded the cities,
marking doors of opportunities
So I could effortlessly walk thru.
While the storms of sweat blinded
the hater and doubters so they could
never get in my way or stop me.
The sweet refreshing fountain of tears, that
quenched my thirst after long hard days
of work, kept me going when my strength
gave out and I thought I wanted to quit.
Yes with you by my side,
The world is mine to have,
Mine to shape as I please.
I will build statues in your honor
So the world may know of you,

And know of your love, and may they
speak for generations of your glory,
Because without you, I would have surely failed...
Indeed it was you my precious, precious woman
It was you, who brought me up...

TERRY LYLE

I am not African;
I am something else

'A letter to the so-called "real" African American'
Mykeal Eternal the Poet Crapper
Baltimore, Maryland/Georgia

No I'm not African, I'm something else

I am the descendant of warriors and freedom fighters, whose begging tongues of "let my people go!" evolved into the demanding tongues of "let freedom ring."

I am the descendant of Harriet Tubman, Fredrick Douglas, Marcus Garvey, Malcolm X, and Martin Luther King.

The very ones that fought against impossible odds and situations, so that I can stand equally with our once oppressors and speak on equal grounds without fear of persecution.

I am the people that came to this country by force, who took it over, and affected the world, forever changing it into our form and image, while you were enslaved and bound in two countries.

I am the Black Panthers, the NAACP, and the Rainbow Coalition.

How dare you come here to my homeland and look down on us and all that was accomplished, so that you yes you, can reap benefits which were never allowed to be enjoyed by my ancestors...

How dare you look down on us with arrogant pride and make your proclamations that we are not African and we are not acknowledged, when we should be praised often for what we have done, and how high we have risen.

You should come here to my homeland with a deep appreciation and respect for the strength we have shown in the face of a mighty enemy.

Us, a people who multiplied, and took over a nation in only a few generations, that should have taken many more.

Us, a people whose walk, talk, dress, and music has transcended races, borders, and countries...

Yet you come with insults, abuse and the very segregated walls that we've fought to destroy for over four decades.

So I say to you... no, I'm not African.

I am something else...

I am evolution...

I am a black man!!!

TERRY LYLE

You bring Joy to me

Karlis N. Wright
New York/Montgomery, Alabama

Baby, you are the Poet in me
That brings the joy you see.
I traveled to get next to you,
Not just to have sex with you.
It's what's bubbling inside that
Feels better than pride.
I Love it when we are together,
Two birds of a feather;
It's like King Kong when he
Looked in her eyes
And began to slip and slide
Just before he died.
You bring joy to me.
Now you can see
Why we can't let this Love just be
So let's let this Love grow
To be the untold,
A Love of a lifetime
As it's now "so" called…

Have I ever been in Love?

Karlis N. Wright
New York /Montgomery, Alabama

You ask me have I ever been in Love.
And I tell you this, this question is ludicrous.
Of course I've been in love with my heart
I thought that we would never ever part.
So full of hope and promise,
Never a doubting Thomas

But life sometimes has a way to say
What kind of fool are you
Man what you gonna do
This girl loves someone else
What will it take for you to see?
I'll never get to the point of bended knees.

Even if her heart were mine
It could not be like the first time

She lives still with a brother
Her body touched by another
Full access at all that ass
Only because he pays for everything cash

So my answer is yes I must attest
I've been in love before
Now my heart is so, so sore
Your constant calling must stop right now
I will no longer be there to put it down
You are but an Attack of the Heart
So deep, so piercing, so please depart.

Feelings Of the Tell, Tell Heart

Karlis N. Wright
New York/Montgomery, Alabama

Women have always been my weakness
Because in them I found my uniqueness.
I'm a special man of sort
Who will avoid being caught.
I'll find no deep love in you,
I'm afraid of being your fool.
This is no reflection on you
It is only what I do.
There is no reason or rhyme why,
You'll never make me cry.
Though my life is full of oh so many smiles
It helps to hide the many miles
Of emptiness in big, big piles.
Life is too short to spend it stressed out
I'd rather be without, no doubt.
I drown my loneliness in flesh
With little or no success.
Even though you maybe better than the rest
You will never measure up or pass my test.
I can never seem to find the right one,

TERRY LYLE

The one in which I would or could succumb.
I will leave you dazed with a stare if you dare.
So you better be prepared or shall I say beware.
You will always wonder about me;
A future with me could never be.
You may wonder or maybe even ponder,
Don't be confused, I won't abuse or misuse.
It's just deep inside I don't want to lose,
So I tell this part,
The feeling of the tell, tell heart.

For the Sake of Love!

Samuel A. Alexander
St. Vincent, Caribbean/ Opelika, Alabama

The suffering is overwhelming! The pain is excruciating! The insult and belittling is over bearing and heart breaking. It is not a dream or a figment of your imagination. It is reality of something just gone badly. You fall into a panic mode, sobbing endlessly. You pick up the pieces and run to the weeping hole, howling in anguish over a painful soul. Rejected and dejected, you weep some more over a painful soul who have just left the shore. You leave the light on burning bright, waiting in the window as you sigh. Why do you do it? You do it for the sake of love.

For the sake of love you suffer the wrong for the right at the hands of family and friends. The insults, ridicules, and mockeries they laid against you, you endure. The constant abuse and misuse of your precious resources you willingly ignore. You stand proud and tall like an oak tree, just to be counted as a tough man for the sake of love.

You spend sleepless nights to soothe and calm a troubled heart, only to be looked upon as a weak emotional freak. You weep and laugh to bring comfort and serenity to a broken spirit. Restlessness overwhelms you as you wander in the midnight hour. Where is the bewildered friend of mine who cannot find his way home in the blackness of darkness? You pace the floor, scratch your head, and cry like an insane man waiting for a run away to call.

You spend what you don't have and go bankrupt to see the love of your life have it all. You grind your teeth; pull your hair, wandering, "How I am going to pay it back?" From the death chamber of unbalanced love, you will do it again for the sake of love.

You trust and splatter your blood. You think of the hurt and want to get even, but you show compassion because you invited him in, just for the sake of love.

So whatever you say! Whatever you do in life! Do it for the sake of love.

Jesus is Knocking

Jeffrey Len Duke
Cincinnati, Ohio

Jesus showed me to myself one night
And all I've been living in.
Then He showed me a great and terrible sight.
This is the consequences for living in sin.

He led me through some tabernacle doors,
That's when I saw His marvelous light.
As I went in, I fell to the floor,
For what I saw was such a beautiful sight.

When I heard of His unconditional love.
Another night, I was so mesmerized,
that I went to the water, to be baptized,
His spirit rained down on me,
From the open Heavens I could see.

But then one night, I kneeled down to pray,
As I reflected on that glorious day,
When he filled me with the Holy Ghost.
I know I'll be a part of His heavenly host.

The Fight

Jim Swettenham
Winnipeg, Manitoba

It happened one night on the Alberta Plain
when two young girls heard something strange.
The girls sat with Pa on the front porch swing
and heard the neighbor say the strangest thing.
For seven long years no rain came down
the land for miles was grayish brown.
There was a color the girls had never seen,
could not even imagine something green.
Most people starved, lived on relief.
Upon the trees was seen not a leaf.
The neighbor said that on that night
God and the Devil were about to fight.
In the sky, God and Devil would clash
the clouds would rumble with lightning flash
and then, as if He were washing sin,
God would cause the rain to begin.
"What is rain?' the girls did pry
as they looked up in the sky.
"Rain is water – a great surprise
that God delivers from the skies."
That is what the neighbors explained
as the girls asked him to tell it again.

"Watch for lightning streaks across the sky.
Listen for thunder, but don't you cry,
for this is how the battle will begin
but do not fear – for God will win."
And then much to their great surprise
water drops washed dust from the skies.
It started slowly, then turned to a flood as dry,
parched earth turned into mud.
The neighbor, their folks and girls did sing
and as at a dance, in the rain, did swing.
The rain continued all the next day
and then the clouds, they rolled away.

The sun came out and begin to shine
and everyone knew they would be just fine.
Grass and weeds and leaves did grow
their prettiest color they did show.
It was the first time, they saw green.
They were so happy the rain did begin
and remembered the words "God will win."

TERRY LYLE

Hurt Pride

Jim Swettenham
Winnipeg, Manitoba

The other day I went to visit my girl,
my head and my heart in such a whirl.
Rode up to her door on my horse,
took her in my arms, of course.
As sure as the suns and the moon do shine,
I want to make that little girl all mine.
My love for her I cannot hide,
want her always by my side.
When I got there her pa wasn't home,
so we were together there all alone.
We knew the moment that her pa pulled up,
heard the barking of his dog and her pup.
I looked out the window, knew I should run,
for her pa was carrying his old shotgun.
He came to the door; I had nowhere to go,
so I jumped out through an open window.
I knew I should run and run really fast,
I heard the gun fire, felt effects of the blast.
I felt the bite as with pellets I'm hit,
back down there where I always sit.
I got to my horse and up in the saddle,
It hurt me to sit, so I had to straddle.

I rode away fast, being chased by the pup,
my feet in the stirrups, I had to stand up.
The worst of my pain was my hurt pride,
worst than the pain where I sit and ride.
But I know that things could have been worse...
I might have rode away in the back of a hearse!

TERRY LYLE

Menopause Meanies

Jim Swettenham
Winnipeg, Manitoba

There is a woman I love so dear -
she actually lives, to me, quite near.
I've known her for most of my life,
for thirty-some years she has been my wife!
There have been times, as of late,
when living with her ain't been that great.
Sometimes she's covered by a rash-
and sometime she ain't,
her outrageous mood swings make me faint.
Of these moods, I've asked the cause,
she say it's something called Menopause.
When it comes to love, I like to get it on,
but dust-like mood quickly switches to dawn,
and then the excuse, "The time is right"-
no matter of morning, noon or at night.
She has seven buddies, I call them the "Meanies"
and in her state she won't wear her bikinis.
At times she is pleasant and then she getsBitchy
she sits and scrathes because she's so Itchy.
Sometimes, like a whale, you'd think she could float,
these are the times she's affected by the Bloat.

One minute she's freezing – then a hot flash.
Off to the bar I tempted to dash…
She switches from ice cold to being so sweaty;
then there are times she's so damn Forgetty.
One minute "I love you" is the key word,
the next minute I'm hated, it's all so absurd.
We'll often sit at evening and talk before bed.
She gets very Sleepy, hears not a thing I have said.
Sometimes it's to a shrink, I think she should go,
she digs in her heels, saying, "I like being Psycho."
Life changes each minute, yes, by the
hour with Meanies on her side,
she has all the power! Maybe she
has, I just stand and glower;
I turn my back and take a cold shower.

TERRY LYLE

Exercise Your Funny Bone

Marlene L. Rameriz- Journalist
Sunshine State of Florida

For many years, researchers have studied laughter's potential health effects on the body. Today, laughter is being used in the medical community as a coping mechanism for stress, as a therapy in pain relief and for recovery from illness. According to research, laughter increases alertness, stimulates the cardiovascular system by increasing oxygen flow; it relieves physical tension, reduces anxiety and reverses stored up anger and frustration. In addition, laughter produces an emotional high. Psychologists say moods are as infectious as the common cold. Here's a "bug" you want to catch.

The Bride and the Groom

The bride tells her husband, "Honey, you know I'm a virgin and I don't know anything about sex. Can you explain it to me first?" "OK, Sweetheart. Putting it simply, we will call your

private place the
prison and call my private thing the prisoner. So
what we do is: put the
prisoner in the prison. And then they
made love for the first time.
Afterwards, the guy is lying face up on
the bed, smiling with satisfaction.
Nudging him, his bride giggles, "Honey
the prisoner seems to have escaped."
Turning on his side, he smiles. "Then
we will have to re-imprison him."
After the second time they spent, the guy reaches for
his cigarettes but
the girl, thoroughly enjoying the new experience of
making love, gives him
a suggestive smile, "Honey, the
prisoner is out again!"
The man rises to the occasion, but with the unsteady
legs of a recently
born fool. Afterwards, he lays back
on the bed, totally exhausted.
She nudges him and says, "Honey,
the prisoner escaped again."
Limply turning his head, He YELLS at her, "Hey,
it's not a life sentence,
OKAY!

TERRY LYLE

No Bikini Lines

Marlene L. Ramirez – Journalist
Sunshine State of Florida

For some women, taking off their bikini top and lying half naked on their beach towel is liberating. Don't forget to rub enough Banana Boat SPF 45 all over your body if you plan on spending the entire day sunbathing unless you want to roast.

The issue is whether you should go topless or not. For the most part, sunbathing topless in South Beach is not surprising. In a recent poll, 66.4% of French women admitted that they felt comfortable about semi-nudity. It's the style in their country so they come to the Sunshine State thinking that it's acceptable to walk along the shore wearing nothing but a white skimpy thong.

During the winter months, women's breasts spend a lot of time hidden underneath furry long coats. With Spring break right around the corner, most women are anxious to take it all off and hopefully get a nice golden tan. If you want a dark tan, stay in the water.

"Nudity on beaches and public places is strictly forbidden," according to the Department of Travel and Tourism. If you are traveling to Florida, you will receive a booklet when you check out at the hotel with all of the Do's and Don'ts. And while America is the land of the free and the home of the brave, topless sun bathing is still forbidden in most beaches with the exception of Haulover Beach. Established by South Florida Free Beaches on July 4, 1991, Haulover Beach Park remains a designated clothing-optional area. For those of you who want to get your freak on, now you know where to visit next time you come to Miami.

According to Florida Statutes 800.03, nudity outside posted area is not permitted. And neither is lewd behavior. So act accordingly and it is a good idea to wear your dark shades if this is the first time you visit this type of establishment. Please be discreet and don't stare at anyone's private parts unless you want to get slapped by a nudist. And before leaving or during your adventure, don't forget to pass by any of the concession stands. Fresh fruits, ice-cream and smoothies are available as well as naturist apparel and books. There's plenty for everyone to do so I am sure that you won't get bored.

Warrior Creed

Obikelvin
Limbe, Cameroon- Africa

The warrior within

The warrior will always be,

The warrior that fights to stay alive,

The warrior that can't break away,

The warrior that wants to be free,

The warrior that will fight for eternity,

The warrior that fights for peace, honor and dignity,

The warrior that is in me can't escape, but pleads and begs for help,

The warrior's creed that will never die.

Giving a Damn

By ObiKelvin
Limbe Cameroon, Africa

I want to erase you from my life and leave not one memory of you imprinted into my mind. I'm exhausted from pushing thoughts of you away as they are shot at me every second of the day. It's sick how much I think of you. I'm obsessed with entertaining the thought you might actually be able to bring yourself to care. I convince myself that I hate you and that I don't want or need you.

Well I try to anyways. I fail miserably every time. I waited for the moment I could be certain that you no longer cared for me. Only then would I be actually able to hate you for leaving me here, alone. Today that moment came. You looked at me while I fought back tears, holding them in just enough. I felt the pressure building as my eyes filled to the brink with tears, and I looked up at you as the first one rolled down my face. You looked at me and the only thing you could offer me was a smile with a slight hint of sympathy, or maybe it was pity. Then you told me you didn't know what to say, that's what hurt the most.

Years of friendship passed, and you had nothing to give me. After pouring out my heart for you, to understand that I couldn't bear the thought of losing you. You had nothing to say to me in return. I knew where I stood. I was no longer needed. I was no longer cared for. I thought once I finally knew that I would hate you. And I do. There's no more needing to convince myself of that. Convincing myself I don't want you around, or need you. I'd hate to know you lay awake at night, contemplating taking your pills, or inflicting pain upon yourself in order to make the aching of your whole body quit.

It's good to know each of your days is not miserable. It's good to know you don't have trouble getting out of bed. It's good to know it doesn't hurt you to live. It's good to know you don't break down at the simple thought of me. It's good to know you don't give a damn that you're killing me. As if I wasn't enough of a head case before, you have completely broken me down. You have ruined me. You broke my trust, and my heart. The sick thing is, if you wanted to ever come back to me, I'd take you in a heartbeat. I loved you always, more than anything. And that is why I hate you for what you've done to me.

Never Leave me Angry

Neva Flores
Columbus, Georgia

When you leave me say goodbye
Always a kiss
Never leave me angry
You must remember this

Angry words they are so hurtful
They cut so deep inside
So never leave me angry
Put aside your pride

Forgiveness is not always easy
But do it in advance
Never leave me angry
You may not have a second chance

TERRY LYLE

Quench

Run your fingers through my hair
As you kiss my lips
Hold me gently in your arms
With your hands upon my hips
Drink me slowly in with each kiss
Take away my air
Teach me to breathe you in
As deeply as I dare
Stir the soul inside of me
Awaken my desire
Mold your body into mine
As you quench my fire

You Just Can't

Lovely Honey
Montreal, Canada

You just can't leave me
On the road all alone
You shall have to come along
That you ought to have known
My love is not shared
With lovers freely blown,
You are the only love
I've ever known.
So come take your share
Be bold,
Be a man
That was your promise
Ere you did behold
And lay me on the floor
As you always did say
May we live?
Happily after this day
Wait now you can't
Leave me all alone
The one I carry
Is not mine alone.

Black Cracker Baseball

Tracy Duke Arnold
Columbus, Georgia

The Georgia Black Crackers are a travelling baseball team, and you might remember them when they were seen, formerly known as the Hurricanes. Most of them started playing when they were T Ball age, now they have matured to a higher grade. Teenage boys who love the game, they give it 100 percent, even in the rain. They practice almost every day, so that on game day, they are ready to play. They have a Short Stop named Isaiah, but they all call him "Zay," boy that little Negro sure knows how to play. The Hind catcher named Joshua was chunky and fat, now that little brother is lean, and can sure swing that bat. Little Sammy is the lead-off batter, and boy let me tell you, his height don't matter. Hanging out at first base is usually Trey, but sometimes he allows his mind to go astray. We usually switch out third with Tiger or Jacorrey, and when you listen to them, they tell some great baseball stories. In left field we have a sharp little brother, Blake Rupp, who else, there is no other. Tyler plays centerfield and sometimes at second, he is fast as a rabbit, and the ball, he can catch it. Antonio catches and pitches as well, when he hits the ball, we just watch it sail. Ayonti can hit the ball and he is usually a sub, but lately he has been showing his skills with his glove. Willie and Trevonne are new additions to the team, so you better watch out when the Black Crackers hit the scene.

The man who they call Coach has been with them the whole time, he is the main reason why the Black Crackers so shine. He has an assistant who help meet the kids' needs, they refer to him as Coach Dorsey. The statistician, who makes the most noise every game, is JMoney, or Janine, that's her name. One other mother whose voice can be heard is Tracy Duke Arnold who stands on the word. Among our parents is a nice little group, Pearlie, Winona, and Mary, bring up the rear of our troop. Sheree has a young son who is lying in wait; he swears he's going to be a Black Cracker some day.

Thanks for stopping by and reading this book. When your friends are watching, don't let them look; tell them go and purchase their own book. Together you can share with the world, the things herein, which got you hooked, while reading this fantastic book!!!

Authoress
Terry E. Lyle

www.ingramcontent.com/pod-product-compliance
Lightning Source LLC
Chambersburg PA
CBHW031144160426
43193CB00008B/242